NOW THAT YOU'VE STOPPED DYING

ESSAYS BY

SEAN PAUL MAHONEY

ZEPHYR BOOKSHELF | COLUMBUS, OH

A limited-edition hardcover is also available from Zephyr Bookshelf.

Cover designed by Jason Lichtenberger.

1 3 5 6 7 8 10

ISBN: 9781074801410

Published by ZEPHYR BOOKSHELF, an imprint of DELIBERATE WIND

*For all the people I get to walk this road with
& for the ones who are no longer around to walk it.*

PREFACE:
UNFINISHED BUSINESS

A PLAY ABOUT two drag queens hosting a bingo night who don't realize they've been killed in a car crash. A novel about unicorns who smoke cigarettes, drink orange soda and live in Los Angeles' Griffith Park. A cookbook-memoir where I cook horrible recipes from celebrity cookbooks and eat them. A gay alcoholic version of Cinderella but like a teen movie. Some novels. Some screenplays. A play about Oscar Wilde in

Colorado, another play about the ghost of Elsa Schiaparelli. These are but a few of the undead creations sitting in that digital limbo known as Google Docs. They're patient, they're hopeful, they're a little delusional. But they hang out there just in case I for some reason decide to unearth them. Just by opening them I give them a false sense of hope that they may someday see the light of day and get to strut their stuff in front of the world. I don't have the heart to delete them, any of them. There's always a tiny chance that I might finish them, but let's get real, finishing isn't really my thing.

I'm no Neil deGrasse Tyson, but I venture to say you could wrap the Earth two times with all the books I didn't finish, Netflix series I have yet to complete and yes, all of the writing projects, large and small that never fully blossomed. I'm removing this veil for myself as a creative person right now, right here in the preface. I have never been that guy who bangs out three books a month and has 5,000 fully completed and realized works of creative genius. If you are looking for that writer, please visit a website entitled Twitter.com. Screw that guy and his mountain of finished works and back patting posts, anyway. Like really, he has another book coming out? Didn't he just released a memoir and sci-fi trilogy last month? I'm so happy for him. On this website, that writer will be easy to find and they will gladly tell you how many books they've written and how awesomely prolific they are. I can assure you that you will see no such tweets in my timeline. Part of my brand as writer is tweet about how many naps I've taken and all the tacos I want to eat. I will not stray from this successful formula. However, my problem with finishing stuff is, of course, deeper in nature than not wanting to be like those pain in the ass writing machines who I am actually jealous of.

A lot of my baggage about not finishing comes from being a drug addict and alcoholic for over 20 years. This is a ridiculous thing to tout, by the way, proudly boasting I was killing myself for two decades as if I was some independent plumber whose commercials you'd see on late night tv. Sean Mahoney: Trying to Numb Out the Pain of Existence Since 1989! Regardless, slowly killing yourself sucks up a lot of time therefore seeing projects to completion wasn't something really within the realm of possibility for me. Okay, sure I could finish a bottle of tequila and polish off a bag of cocaine; beyond that, you were out of luck. College degrees, large novels I always wanted to read, lofty personal goals like saving money or calling people back, all got tossed onto the "to be done" later pile. But that pile never gets done and the more wasted I got, the more got added to it. Eventually, even the idea of getting sober got thrown on there too. I had some awareness that maybe, just maybe, not doing drugs and drinking everyday might be a good thing. I'd even seen people in my universe get sober and they seemed happy. I mean boring, but happy. Yet it seemed like a lot of work. I had tried in a lot of half-ass ways to get sober on my own and without fail after a few months, I would fizzle out. I always still felt horrible, alone and wanting to drink and use. Right on cue, I'd start all over again. It was unceremonious.

There were no big gasps from concerned family or friends. I kept the expectations on my sobriety to a minimum. I downplayed that I was even attempting it because I think I knew on some level that the whole thing wouldn't be successful. Sort of like when they tried bring back Melrose Place; it was like, "Hey, here it is but manage your expectations because it won't last, okay?" Therefore, when I did start drinking again there weren't a lot of raised eyebrows and heads shaking. It just felt inevitable. Like, of course I didn't stay sober. I reaped the appropriate rewards for not really trying. But in 2009 when things were categorically shitty and off the charts awful, I actually gave it a shot. I finally noticed the neon sign flashing above my head, visible to the rest of the planet. My way of life wasn't working. Basically, I was in enough pain to try something else. I then did what lots of other people do who try to get sober. I went to all the meetings. I cried all of the time. I looked at all the horrible, malfunctioning ways I operated as a human being and tried to change them. I asked for help five billion times and my prideful, delusional ass hated every moment of it. I even started to feel better and change, a little bit at a time. Nevertheless, there was a nagging fear that I wouldn't make it, that I wouldn't stay sober, that sobriety this time around would be another thing I couldn't and wouldn't finish. When I made it to six months, I couldn't believe it. The most time I ever had sober was five months and that "may" have involved popping some pills and smoking weed. But this six months was legit and it felt unreal. Later, when I got to nine months, a sober friend of mine said, "You gave birth to a big, gay, adult sober baby!" It felt that way. I didn't know who I was. This new person was not at all like that guy who couldn't finish things. Yet on some level I still had my doubts.

At 11 months sober, I remember sitting in a meeting in Santa Monica and crying. Here I was with nearly a year clean and sober, actually sober - no weed, no pills, no misused Benadryl - yet I still felt like shit. Like legit garbage. Oh, I was sober, but the rest of my life was a disaster. I had no money. My health sucked. I was lonely. I was back in school and it was hard and it reminded me why I didn't finish it the first go round. None of this made any sense. Here I was honestly avoiding the things that were slowly killing me and undoubtedly ruining my life but everything still sucked. I remember blubbering at that meeting, "I can't believe I got sober for this." Also at 11 months, there was still a feeling in the pit of my stomach that I wouldn't make it to a year. After all, I'm the guy who doesn't finish anything. There was no way a person like me, who used drugs and drank since 1989, would make it to a year sober. Why even bother? It would be very expected for me to go out. Everybody knew how hard my year had been so it might not even be that big of a deal. Maybe people would shrug their shoulders and it wouldn't really be discussed. What's more is maybe I'd find a way to make that way of life work again? Maybe I'd find the secret way to balance drinking and drugs that wouldn't make me a total nightmare? Despite not feeling that great and sort of hating everything, I somehow stuck around. I hung in there even though I felt like I was going to leave and never be a year sober.

When I picked up my one year sober chip, I burst into tears. I did it. I made to a year. Life would all get easier. The money, the jobs, the men. It would all come now that I finished something and made it to a year!

Uh. Yeah. That did not happen. In fact, almost everything got harder. I was a person who avoids feelings, responsibilities and yes, finishing anything and so now that I was sober all of it was waiting for me. Everything I didn't want to deal now had to be dealt with. Terrific. This felt at direct conflict from what people, films and books were saying. I was promised a shiny, easier sober life, dammit . This sober life that I got was hard, messy and kind of a shit show. I wanted a refund and needed to speak to the manager. Who knew that dealing with life without something (or a lot of somethings) to take off the edge would be this hard?

This is what I started writing about, back in 2011. I had two years sober and didn't know it was all going to be so damn difficult. I was getting paid to write random blog posts and web content and was basically grateful to be alive and doing something I loved my whole life. In the meantime, me and a small group of folks blogged about what it was like to stay sober. We connected. We liked each other's posts. We commented. We laughed. A lot. But it wasn't the heavily sponsored, click baity digital world of recovery today. Just some drunks and addicts sharing their stories. Lots of other people found my work during this time frame too: Normal drinkers, people with mental illness, and for some reason, a niche audience of people who suffered from traumatic brain injuries, even though I don't have a TBI. The TBI people were very courageous with big senses of humor. It's not lost on me that a person like myself who tried on his own to destroy his brain learned a lot from people who overcame their own neurological challenges. I am extremely grateful for all the sober people I met online during that time too. We were little lighthouses in the electronic void and we bleeped and flashed our spotlights so we wouldn't feel alone. I mainly wrote about being sober but still feeling kind of awful. I wrote about trying to figure out how to grow spiritually while still hating everyone. Mainly, I tried to write honestly about where I was.

I have struggled with honesty my whole life as an addict, so my blogs were a way to come clean. I would even like to say that they helped me embrace the truth about who I am, but even that wouldn't be 100% honest. Embracing honesty sounds hard and potentially smelly, like I don't want to embrace anything that isn't warm cuddly and a total escape. Thus, the best I can say is blogging helped me move closer to the truth, which is also the name of a decent Cher record.

Luckily, it's been a journey that others are on too. Turns out life didn't magically get better for people who successfully quit drinking. Trying to tell the truth one blog post at a time, one essay at a time, has connected me to other writers, readers and people in recovery around the globe. The weirdest, saddest, most beautiful chapters of our collective lives were happening after hitting bottom and thank god we had each other to share it with.

All of this leads us to where you are now: reading this book. Basically 40-some essays about me rambling about trying to stay sober while dropping as many pop culture references as possible, I hope this book is really about what happens next. What happens next is a life that's messy, sad, hilarious and certainly unfinished.

PART I

ALL THOSE THINGS
I FORGOT TO DO

UNIQUELY QUALIFIED

WE WANTED TO try the drug that killed River Phoenix. Of course we were devastated by the loss of such a young talent who already, in his short time in films, meant so much to people in my generation. Of course it was a huge tragedy and we all felt really bad for the Clan Phoenix: Leaf, Rainbow, Summer, *et al.* Of course we knew nothing about GHB or how it worked or why everyone was suddenly taking it. We just wanted to try it despite it playing a role in the death of River Phoenix.

Now, I'm not sure this is a thought that normal people, who aren't human drug dumpsters, would have. Smart money would say that these people probably think, "That drug killed a man! No thank you, sir!" Yet I am not smart people; I'm sure the fuck not normal people. I wanted to try it. I didn't want to feel like there was some chemical that made people forget about their lives that I hadn't tried. Fear of missing out on oblivion. FOMOO. So what if it killed them? Thus me and a bunch of I'm sure what could be described as other non-normal people set out and tried GHB. We did it in a bathroom at a rave in Denver, Colorado and unlike when River Phoenix did it, there were no headlines. It was just drugs in a bathroom at a rave in

Denver, Colorado. It was exactly as unceremonious, very 90's and slightly depressing as it sounds. The thing about GHB, it was totally underwhelming. Unlike ecstasy which I had done boatloads of and did so much of it that it stopped working entirely, GHB was unmemorable. It sort of felt like cocaine for people who liked to take too much cold medicine and enjoyed the sensation of just stepping off a Tilt a Whirl. Like I said, underwhelming. Naturally, I did it about 40 more times over the course of my drug taking career. You know, just to be sure I didn't like it.

Speaking of that drug taking career, a career that is low paying but easy to get into, mine is vast. I feel like this is important to mention as a person who writes about addiction. Julia Child knows what she's talking about when she talks about roasting a chicken because that bitch went to Le Cordon Bleu. Likewise, Andre Leon Talley sat through 65,000 runway shows and therefore, I'd imagine we can trust him when he talks about fashion. All of which is to say, I'd like to reassure you that you're in capable hands when I talk to you about drinking and taking drugs. Not that this is all that impressive. I'm just the rare person with this career who didn't get killed by it or who isn't still doing it. Nevertheless, you can trust me when I talk about this stuff. Well, as much as you can trust any alcoholic or addict. That's the thing I find really funny; we get pissed off at people like James Frey for lying about the extremes of their alcoholism. We were outraged! Oprah was outraged! But hello, he's an alcoholic. We lie. That's just what we do. The stories of fisherman catching whales are more reliable than any story from a drunk and if Hemingway is to be believed they're all drunks too so there you go.

Also? If you're really great at this career like I am, you probably drank enough and used enough drugs to not remember most of the details. Therefore, you'd have to fill it in with all kinds of wild bullshit to make it interesting. Like factory work at the turn of the century, a robust drinking or using career is pretty mundane and depressing. It's just one miserable attempt to use chemicals to wipe out reality after the next. Sure, you might barf on yourself, offer a random cab driver a blow job while in a black out and watch a drunk guy's glass eye fall out of his head, all in one evening, but really it all blurs together in one sad unmemorable montage. Basically, you have my word that I when I talk to you about my drinking and using I will not lie and won't talk about things I don't actually remember. Are you happy now, Oprah?

My humble career started with smoking Marlboro Reds with a chick named Tanya at age 14 on the way to junior high in Golden, Colorado. Drinking was not too far behind starting with vodka orange juice, a Smith cassette, a kid named Chance and vomiting in the snow. Pot came later, which was followed by taking acid, then cocaine and then mushrooms all by the tender age of 17. I was in the accelerated program. While you were wasting your time in AP English, I was skipping school and taking acid with some skater guy named Mark who I wanted to make out with but didn't actually realize I wanted to make out with him until later. At 16, I took ecstasy for the first time and jumped on the trampoline in my backyard with a kid named Courtney, who I also wanted to make out with. I thought it was funny that I did cocaine at gay bars I was too young to be in because a.) I wasn't out of the closet and my parents would lose their shit if they found out and b.) My dad was literally a police officer on the Narcotics Bureau, busting cocaine dealers at the time. Insert a lot more teen drinking and drugs taking all before I sort of graduated. By graduated, I mean my "maybe" lesbian ceramics teacher helped me earn my missing credits by letting me clean up the studio after school. There's also an arrest for stealing booze with the aforementioned kid named Chance. He had such a lucky name for such an unlucky kid, to be friends with a teenage tsunami like myself. We were slapped on the hand and forced to do some alcohol classes or some bullshit which, obviously really worked.

This is all before I even turned 21, mind you. I'll save us all some time and say that ecstasy at raves led to meth at raves, which led to actual legal drinking, which led to more meth, which finally led to me moving to Los Angeles. Sensing something was not okay, my older brother gently suggested that I move to Los Angeles and stay with him. It was 1995, what possible trouble could a drug addict and burgeoning alcoholic like myself possibly get into? Plenty would be the correct answer. Before you knew it, a healthy club going life turned into a dive bar life, which turned into a seven nights a week drinking at home life for the last 6 years of my illustrious career. By the time I turned 36, I had racked up over 22 years of drinking. It felt like a good moment to "retire" as it were.

Other notables I guess would include a onetime only stint with heroin. For some odd reason, it was the one drug that didn't stick. I did it in a warehouse with some random jewelry designers who all shot it up while I did it as drops in my nose. They barfed their guts out and would later become junkies while I laid still on the floor of the warehouse and tired not to vomit as visions of Jesus coming down from a UFO with lasers in his eyes polluted my brain. This was maybe the one moment in my career where I actually said, "I don't have to do that ever again!" Special K or Ketamine or cat tranquilizer, however, was more on trend with how I did drugs. Sure, I hated it and it made me feel like I wanted to poop while being trapped underwater, but I for some reason, did it a bunch of times. It was usually with drag queens and in nights that wound up in some combination of confusion or tears or both, K was a drug I just kept giving the old college try. Like maybe this time I could really make a cat tranquilizer be successful for me! It never was and after having it at a Grammy party at my house which caused a few of my guests to puke and lose their minds, I hung up my Ketamine boots for good. Ketamine Boots is also the name of my electronic band, by the way. Who serves Special K at a Grammy party anyway? Whatever happened to Seven Layer Dip? My last time with mushrooms was at Jumbo's Clown Room, a strip club in Hollywood. If I have to explain why a sad strip club and hallucinogens is a terrible idea, then maybe you should stop reading right now. When I turned 28, I took ecstasy and sat on the beach in Malibu and had a rare moment of "Maybe this is great and I should quit while I'm ahead with this drug?" After all, I had done it for over 10 years and certainly rode it until the wheels fell off and miraculously came back on. It felt like a rare moment of self-control and one that I should run with. As far as pills go, they weren't really my thing. Sure, I popped not-prescribed-to-me-but-prescribed-to-someone Xanax on more than one occasion and I used to take Vicodin with a guy named Tim who worked at a bar where I worked who I didn't want to make out with but I would have if the situation had come up. It was fantastic mixed with a lot of booze and made me feel like Elizabeth Taylor, but it was pre-opioid epidemic and hard to get, so all roads eventually led back to alcohol and cocaine. Preferably lots of both.

Right before I hit rock bottom, there was a night at my house (the house that I was about to get evicted from), I snorted damn near an eight ball of cocaine with a bunch of friends. Said friends were listening to music and laughing like you do on a night of cocaine and drinking. I, on the other hand, sucked up the cocaine like an aardvark with a pile of ants and announced I was going to bed. Clearly, it had stopped working. The following months when I would do it, it would give me panic attacks. Same with drinking. It stopped doing what I wanted it to do in the first place: numb out my life.

It's a low point in a drinking career when you can't get drunk and when you do, you still feel the pain of existence. What a rip off. All I really accomplished in this two decades long career was hating myself, losing my mind and wanting to die. When I got sober, I was not thanked for my dedication. There was no cake. There was no party. There was no gold watch.

Now I gladly share my experience with you with the fucked up knowledge that there is actually still more I could add to my resume if I really wanted to. I've been sober long enough to see Moscow Mules come and go out of fashion. I never even had the chance to sip out of metal cup with hipsters. However will I survive? I've never gotten sloppy drunk on Rosé. Who knew if I stayed sober long enough, I'd entirely miss an era where bros got proudly tore up on cheap pink wine? I was also never a successful crack smoker (if there is such a thing.) I mean, I tried it bunch of times and it didn't work so I could always try harder. "I've never even had a Four Loko!" he cries like most older white ladies in the Midwest cry, "I've never even been to Italy!"

I completely missed the craft beer revolution. I mean was it a revolution? Were there actual battles? Were there uniforms? Like I said, I missed it. I also never got to try synthetic drugs like elephant tranquilizer or scary ass shit like Flaca, which is probably on par with the GHB of yesteryear, but now you can film how stupid you look on it and post it on YouTube. As enjoyable as drinking a Moscow mule and doing Flaca in a field somewhere at age 45 sounds, I think retirement suits me. I live a life currently where I usually know where my keys are and who I texted the night before. I don't get thrown out of places or arrested. But mainly I no longer read that a drug killed someone and think, "Ooh! I should try that!"

MY BOTTOM IS
A WONDERLAND

"AT THE LOWEST possible level." That's how the wonderful internet defines the term "rock bottom." So like the Star Wars prequels? Maybe lower than that. Maybe it's more like the film career of Shaquille O'Neal? Still lower, perhaps. Maybe the idea of McDonald's McPizza served with an iced cold Crystal Pepsi? I still think we can go a few levels lower. How about being such a dumpster fire of an alcoholic or drug addict that your whole world implodes? Now we're talking "lowest possible level" and an idea of rock bottom that I can really relate to.

You hear people talking a lot about their bottoms in the halls of recovery. Before we go any further, let's get the 6th grade snicker about the word "bottom" out of the way. I am here with you on that and am resisting making obvious childish butt jokes. We can stay strong together and avoid 1,500 words of bottom puns. It'll be hard but we can do it. Anyway, you hear people talk about their bottoms a lot (tee-hee-hee. already failing.) if you are like me and hang out with sober people several times a week. It almost always comes up in meetings. In case you're unfamiliar, your "rock bottom" is a way to legitimize our experiences as former alcoholics and drug addicts. It's like confirmed kills or teardrop tattoos for gangsters, but with stories of vomiting in public and peeing yourself instead. When we share our bottoms with each other (extreme snicker required) it's supposed to unite our experiences and highlight what we have in common. We're supposed to nod our heads and think to ourselves, "Oh my god, I did that shit too." Looking at our bottoms together (oh good lord) should unite us in the idea that we all come from fucked up places when we drag our sorry selves into the halls of recovery. It should, and more often than not, it does but there are a lot of times when comparing bottoms (I give up) does nothing but make things worse.

Blow up my darn email or post some comments on my website if you feel the need, but I am of the particular belief that there is no such thing as a low bottom or high bottom. The very notion does nothing but create division within a group of people who already feel like massive hunks of garbage. Alcoholism and addiction don't care if it's high or low bottom. As far as the people who love us and who've had to put up with our bullshit are concerned, it's all low bottom. Still, we sober folks feel like we need to let everybody know what our bottoms are like, inside and out.

If you cling to this idea of being a high bottom, for example, you feel the need to share every time that you open your mouth at a meeting that things never got that bad and you never lost all of your stuff. You feel like everybody needs to know that you don't have to be a hobo to get sober and that you can still drive your DUI-free BMW to meetings. Thanks for sharing that, Donna, but if things never got that bad then why the hell are you in recovery? I have met some first class wackadoodles with major cases of alcoholism who looked pretty darn shiny from the outside. Remember, I got sober in Los Angeles. The foundation of that entire town is built on people who look good on the outside but are collapsing internally. This leads me to believe the insides of drug addicts and alcoholics are all the same. We all hate ourselves. We all made disasters of our lives even if nobody could tell. Mainly, we all couldn't stop drinking and using once we started. This highbrow ideal that we were a class act when we got bombed is the exact kind of delusion that kept me loaded in the first place.

You're not off the hook either, super low bottom drunks. As entertaining as that story you have about smoking crack with a rat under a bridge when you were homeless is, Travis, it wears a little thin. I mean, we get it. You once set yourself on fire when you passed out drunk with a lit cigarette. What else ya got? Super braggy low bottoms want to let you know that they were the worst kind of alcoholic ever and you shouldn't even bother trying to compete with them. In actuality, it's the same damn thing. If you get to hang out with enough addicts and alcoholics, the one thing you'll see over and over again is that their thinking is all selfish, self-destructive and totally nuts. With low bottom drunks more often than not, the conversation verges into all war stories all the time which makes me a little bored and start wondering, "Yeah okay, but then what happened?"

As what could be considered a low bottom drunk myself, I admittedly have often rolled my eyes when people share about drinking because they didn't have the grades they wanted when they went to Yale or getting fucked up because the stock market took a dump. I used to snort cocaine off the backs of gay bar toilet seats and had no shame in drinking Steel Reserve, so instinctively I want to snap, "I can't relate." The reality is, though, I can relate. Maybe not to the situations or circumstances but to the feelings simmering underneath. When people are real and raw, the hair on the back of my neck stands up. My head nods for real and to my core, I hear someone telling my story.

The first time this happened to me I was at a meeting in Santa Monica. It was an early morning meeting at a coffee shop filled with good looking, high bottom types. The woman who spoke, shared about being a studio wife and driving around Brentwood picking up her kids while drunk. My single, gay ghetto ass from Echo Park couldn't be more different but when she talked about always feeling less than, feeling alone in crowds of people and wanting to kill herself but being too afraid, she said everything that had been on my mind for decades. She said she never, ever thought she'd be able to stop but now had three years. I felt that way too and at less than 30 days sober, it meant something coming from a total stranger, regardless of our respective zip codes.

When I think about my own bottom today (I'll allow one more groan and a light titter), it's pretty clear cut. It was bad. Moreover, it was bad enough. It was bad enough to make me stop and think, "This isn't working." Granted, given the number of years I drank and used for, I probably had a series of little baby bottoms, but none of them were bad enough. However, the one in 2009 where I lost everything (internally and externally, by the way) was. I felt spectacularly shitty enough to consider something, anything else. An impulse to save my own life from somewhere kicked in. An out of character surge of self-preservation and desperation took over. My bottom was horrific and awful enough for me to stop and finally ask for help, which in the end, is all that really matters.

I WON'T RUIN YOUR BARBECUE. YOU'RE WELCOME.

FOR THE EIGHTH Fourth of July in a row, I will not ruin your barbecue. As much as I know you'd like me to show up at your dignified, patriotic while still being kitschy backyard fiesta, I will not. This means I won't arrive at your function already buzzed even though it's only 2pm. Ditto, I won't fall down in your entryway at 5pm. And, finally, I won't sneak away from the party to send a series of crazy text messages trying to find cocaine. I know you're disappointed, but that's the way it is.

See, the summer of 2008, I used up more than my share of "Hot Mess in the Middle of the Afternoon" coupons. There was a series of backyard summery jamborees hosted by my best friend and at all of them, I was the biggest mess in the room. This is a feat because outside of a Barrymore family reunion, never has there been a group who can drink their faces off like this group. Nevertheless, this was the summer where my drinking went from festive to horribly sad in about 60 seconds. A friend at one of these get-togethers even remarked, "Wow. Sean, every time I see you at one of these things, you're pretty drunk." This was a friend who'd been jailed on drug charges, so she knew what she was talking about.

Now, I was a good guest on paper. You'd invite me for my witty banter. You'd invite me for promptness and ability to help out in the kitchen. And even if you didn't love me for my personality, you loved me for my potato salad, which, by the way, is pretty rock star. I take particular pride in my white person culinary abilities to nail all of your mom-type mayonnaise based salads (chicken, egg, macaroni, potato, what-have-you). But as the shitstorm of alcoholism becomes a category 5, it ain't all cheeky jokes and deviled eggs. Soon after a few drinks, you were always checking your watch and wondering when I'd leave. To my credit, I was never a yeller or a drunken crier. I was more the politely drink myself into a coma type of guest. Messy for sure, but contained messy. Well, at least until that summer.

One barbecue, which could have been Fourth of July but who knows really, stands out as the deal breaker. What my hard drinking friends didn't know was that I usually "pregamed" the drinking before I even got there. You know, just one large ass tumbler of vodka and something to really loosen me up. This means I was probably "half in the bag" before I got there. Or maybe I was fully in the bag? Is that something we even say? Now that I'm sober, does that mean I'm out of the bag? Who knows. The truth was, I was buzzed before I got there and rapidly I got even drunker. Disproportionately drunk for the time of day and progress of the party, mind you.

Amazingly, I somehow always knew when I had crossed over or I was about to cross over. I somehow had some drunken forethought about when I needed to get the hell out of dodge. The pull of being a people pleaser is a powerful one, friends. It was fine that I was the drunkest person in the room. I just didn't want to look like the drunkest person in the room. At this barbecue, those instincts once again kicked and I had to go.

As I was trying to leave, knowing that I was wasted and had to get out before it got even worse, I took a tumble-down some concrete stairs. These were the typical bungalow-style outdoor entryway steps that look cute but can turn into scab makers if approached while intoxicated. The fall itself was an awkward backslide down steps resembling Michael Douglas and

Kathleen Turner's iconic mudslide from Romancing the Stone yet somehow messier. I bounced on the cement, only to be stopped by the metal security door at the foot of the steps. Two or three people propped me up, dusted me off and gladly pushed me onto the street. The hangover, the scraped up hand and the throbbing, bruised tailbone were unbearable. I woke up more humiliated than usual. It was painful on lots of levels, but mainly because I had five months sober. I say had because until May of 2008, I had patched together five months of sobriety with no help, no support and no clue that when life happened (which it did and always does), I would go to my only coping mechanism - booze. In the summer when my literal fall from grace occurred, I was still writing things in my journal like, "I'm drinking again but I think I've figured out how to control it" or "I'm drinking again but it's really not a huge deal." I was clinging onto my drinking and my red solo cup, hoping that I could control myself at barbecues but deep inside I knew better. Oddly, that tumble during that barbecue that could have been on the Fourth of July was a big catalyst in me getting sober. The shame of limping into the street and waking up sore stayed with me. I was tired of being that person at the party. Slowly, I started to wonder if maybe it was big deal. But it took being shitfaced waiting tables on Halloween and blacking out a few days before Christmas for me to get it. By January 2009, the party, backyard or otherwise, was finally over.

Even with as much time as I have sober now, I still flinch at party invitations. I don't believe in showing up to lame bullshit parties just because people want me there. If it's just some fools tasting one another's craft cocktails while I roll my eyes with a Diet Coke, then my behind will stay on the sofa. My mental list of questions for a party attendance is as follows, "Will there be other sober people there?" "Is there an activity happening other than just me watching people getting hammered at said function?" and most importantly, "For the love of God, is there food at this damn thing?" If the answer is no to one or more of these questions, I have to politely decline.

So no, I won't be able to make it to your daytime drinking, grillin' and chillin' Fourth of July extravaganza. It's better off this way. I'm better off this way... but, I'll totally make potato salad sometime if you want.

IT SEEMED LIKE A GOOD
IDEA AT THE TIME

HUMAN BEINGS ARE capable of many wonderful things. But mainly we're really great at generating some truly horrible ideas. Yes, we the people are filled to the brim with great innovations and life changing ideas too. Yet, for every polio vaccination, there are 100 films remade with the Rock and 3,000 truckloads of Doritos Locos Tacos. Lots of times, we special little beings have no idea that our ideas are awful. Maybe we don't figure it out until later. Maybe it's not until we troll the Facebook page of the crazy person we used to date that we know how truly bad some of our ideas are. But I think there's a lot of ideas we have that we know are bad in the moment, but we do them anyway. Maybe some of us just naturally produce shitty ideas with little to no effort at all.

Take me, for example. I, myself, have had some earth shatteringly bad ideas in my over 40-years on this Earth. From wearing acid wash to falling in love with unavailable, straight, meth addicts, my bad ideas are as majestic as the Grand Canyon and as puzzling as the film career of Jennifer Lopez. Perhaps I was born under a bad idea sign because as far back as I can remember, I've cooked up one harebrained plot after the next only to have it backfire and explode in my face. As an early forger of report cards and author of book reports on titles that never existed, the shittacular schemes knew no bounds. I was also totally down to be an accomplice to your bad ideas if you needed such a service. I'm thoughtful like that. After all, I wouldn't let you take acid during math class alone. Petty theft, lying about medical conditions to get sympathy, inventing romances with people who don't exist? I've done all of those things and they were all categorically horrific ideas that spectacularly backfired in my face. If there's a Bad Idea Museum, I'm quite certain I'm a shoo-in for the curator position.

The anatomy of bad ideas, as far as I can tell, stems from the corny "live and learn" concept. We have awesomely horrific ideas, we experience hell on Earth because of them and we never, ever have those ideas again. Poof! It's that easy. You fucked up and you never fucked up like that again. Yet live and learn is some impossible bullshit for addicts like me who live by the "This time for sure!" Bullwinkle approach to bad ideas. Like, let's try a few more times just to make sure it's actually a bad idea.

If the "live and learn" concept was one I adapted, I would have only fallen in love with just the one unavailable, straight, drug addict. Not four. My hands down worst ideas were always the ones I tried a few times just to make sure they didn't work, the biggest being spending my rent money on drugs and alcohol instead of paying rent. My brilliant idea was that maybe my great personality would help my landlords see that I'd pay it eventually and maybe they should give me a free month or two until I got it together. Sounds reasonable, right? Well, apparently not and thanks to a few evictions, I can now tell you that landlords in general are not cool with this idea. Go figure!

Anyway, when it came to drugs and drinking, the ideas, which were already being cooked up in a crappy idea kitchen, were escalated to new hilariously awful heights when I was loaded. There was the time I shimmied across the gangsta tin awning, which hung over my neighbor's blind and endlessly barking dog, en route to my open bathroom window where my tequila soaked body landed in the bathtub, all in an effort to break into my own house. I had forgotten my keys and my best idea was to shove my drunken butt through a tiny window. In this case, the initial idea wasn't that awful as I did accomplish the goal of getting in my house. However, it was unfortunate to discover the next day that my front door was unlocked the entire time, meaning my Touchstone film comedy-style break-in was totally pointless.

Another favorite terrible idea of mine went down went I used to DJ at a club in Hollywood. That's an incredibly douchey sentence, which I'm sure sounds like a cool job with glamorous people. Really it's an okay job where you spend a surprising amount of time telling drunk girls that you don't have any Puff Daddy. But one night when I was DJing, a friend walked by and handed me a pill. No questions asked or even a preview from the friend that this pill was coming, I just popped it in my mouth. Later as I started to feel head scrambled, I thought, "What was that, anyway?"

I never found out, but I can guess it was some sort of opioid that poor white ladies in Cincinnati are now hopelessly hooked on. The sober, not on a mission to die, version of me clearly sees popping a strange unidentified pill into his mouth as a bad idea. Without my bad ideas, I'm not very fun and what's more, I still don't have any Puff Daddy.

Sadly, I cannot report that sobriety has entirely cured me from bad ideas. Marry someone and they will be sure to let you know that this is true. My dear husband Michael is on the tail end of most of my bad ideas today. At least the current crop of bad ideas are of the "watching a season of Sense8" variety and not the "breaking into my own home drunk" type. I sometimes even have a brilliant notion to call someone when I think an idea might be terrible. This person, whoever they are, is usually quick to confirm that my idea is garbage. Ideas like having a buttload of dark chocolate before I go to bed or chiming in with an opinion when nobody asked for it, might be the kind of bad ideas I keep repeating. Once you're born under a bad idea sign, it's hard to shake yourself free of them entirely. However, I can say that the idea of staying sober that I had in 2009 turned out to be a good one.

NOW THAT YOU'VE STOPPED DYING

NOW THAT YOU'VE stopped dying, you should probably figure out what to do. I mean no pressure or anything, but maybe you should talk about what happens next?

If this were a Sondheim musical, I'd tell you to pop your butt up on a piano, thrust your leg out of the slit in your gold sequin dress and sing Being Alive in B flat.

If it were a 1950's Douglas Sirk film, I'd tell you to shout, "I want to live!" right before Rock Hudson passionately kisses you and the credits roll. Worse still, if this was 2017 I'd tell you that now that you've stopped killing yourself, you should turn your survival into a lifestyle brand starting with inspirational memes and followed by pricey spa retreats. But it's none of those things. In fact, I'm not even talking about you; I'm talking about me.

Here's the thing, and there is no snappy, user friendly way around what I'm about to say: I was dying for the better part of 20 years. No, I wasn't hooked up to machines, constantly buzzing and beeping out auditory beacons to my loved ones. Nor was I battling a crippling disease that they hold star-studded telethons for. I'm "just" an alcoholic and an addict with mental illness, which is sort of like saying "just" an atom bomb or "just" a reality show host in the White House. Nevertheless, the goal of what I have and the diseases that others have is the same. They want you dead. It's not personal, it's just what life threatening illnesses do. Yet, somehow I outran these pesky little fuckers who wanted to kill me. What's more, is over time, I somehow pieced together a decent amount of sobriety as well as treating the other various and sundry illnesses that also aren't too keen on me hanging around. Kudos to me. I'll sing a rousing version of "No One is Alone" the black velvet curtain will close and everyone leaves filled with hope and that's it.

Yet what I and millions of other who have survived addiction, alcoholism and other fatal delights can tell you is that isn't it. That's far from it. In fact, now that you've stopped killing yourself, the party's just beginning. And I don't necessarily mean "party" in the sense of silver balloons and mini quiches. I mean the "Holy fuck. What did I sign up for?" type of party. It's this very sensation (a sensation that I can tell you nearly nine years into the sobriety game does not go away) is why we probably don't talk about what happens after you've stopped dying. It's too painful, too intense, too much of slog; life on the other side of death is a fucking mess. We don't talk about it because god forbid we scare someone off from getting sober with stories of endlessly handling our bucket of crazy. We don't talk about it because it's complicated. It doesn't fit this American ideal of recovery, one that tells you to take a pill or get a treatment, get better and never speak of it again. It doesn't vanish or stop being life threatening and all the positive affirmations in the world won't change that. Mainly, I don't think we talk about it because now that you've stopped dying things can get really hard. But maybe we should?

The thing is, you don't just survive once or surrender once. You have to do it all of the time, darling. Like I said, that's a drag to hear. Nevertheless, it's true and there's so much you can look forward to. Particularly with addiction and alcoholism, one of the delights you get to deal with is the backlog of never ending emotions. So unlooked at and downright ignored, the mountain of unprocessed emotions make the inbox of my rarely used Hotmail account seem manageable. One of my goals as an addict was to never feel anything. It was a goal I gladly met and even exceeded. Come to think of it, I should have received a promotion, I was so good at it. Yet like any good creditor, emotions wanted me to pay double when I finally faced them.

Not only did I cry for five months solid when I first got sober, but I finally experienced fear, sadness, rage, elation and compassion. See, I told you it was a party. A party at Mary Todd Lincoln's house, but a party nonetheless. Somewhere in the middle of my seventh year sober, I was delighted to learn that I could now experience several house-shaking emotions all at the same time. For a guy who has difficulty watching Netflix while doing laundry, this feat of multi-tasking is impressive. Yet there I was. I was grieving a death while feeling extreme joy for personal success and all the while feeling concerned for people in my life who were hurting too. I came out on the other side of that year, the captain of tiny ship who figured out how to hang to my boat without the ocean of emotions tipping it over.

Now that you've stopped dying, the other thing you can expect to routinely fail at is handling normal life stuff. Beyond emotions, there's all the other things you need to do that you didn't do while you were dying. From taxes and calling people back to finally seeing a doctor about that thing on your chin, there's no shortage of stuff to handle. Cracked teeth, annoyed relatives awaiting phone calls and pets in dire need of a vet visit all need attending to and now that you can form sentences and stand up for more than 20 minutes, you're just the person to do it. These things have piled up and more are on the way, so no need in killing yourself (again) to try and get to them all.

Now that you've stopped dying, you have another gift waiting for you. Time. All of those hours you spent hung over, wanting to die or chasing down your next high have reappeared. You suddenly have hours upon hours of time, but what the hell do you do with them? If you're crafty, I suppose you could take all of your non-dying time to perfect decoupage or macramé. You could just go crazy watching the clock and pace back and forth. Cue up Losing My Mind and light up a cigarette.

What most of us do is hang out with each other. Because now that we've all stopped dying-we alcoholics, we addicts, we people with mental illness-we need something. We need something to make us feel okay since we have to feel stuff nowadays and as far as I can tell, the only thing that does that is other people who have also almost died. We are statistical anomalies. We are freaks of nature. We are former zombies who now have to mix in with people who were living normally all along. If we travel in a huddle, we are okay and we aren't alone. We don't know what's next and honestly it doesn't matter. I mean we survived worse. So you whistle "I'm Still Here", you grab your coat and meet other friends like you for coffee. You might as well. What else can you do, now that you've stopped dying?

ALL THOSE THINGS YOU FORGOT TO DO

I FORGOT I had teeth. I forgot that teeth needed to be taken care of. I forgot that teeth could only handle so many cigarettes, so many sugar bombed shots of alcohol and so many light dustings of cocaine. I forgot that teeth will let you know that you've abused them and when they do, it will not be pretty. I quickly remembered all of this around my third year of sobriety.

My teeth, the poor neglected bastards, staged a revolt. A revolting revolt, at that. It went from gums that hurt a little to the entire row of front lower teeth trying to pull away and angrily leave my mouth as if they were upset moviegoers who had finally had it with Kevin Hart. Yes, four wanted to leave and wanted to leave at the same time. With the bleeding, swelling and general horribleness they caused my mouth, I wanted them to leave too. They hurt to touch, to look at, and fuck even trying to brush. They needed to go, meaning I needed to go to the dentist, something I hadn't done in forever. It was all something I had just forgotten to do.

When the life goal of drugs and alcohol is to never feel anything ever, forgetting just comes with the territory.

For me, it's a chicken and egg kind of thing. Did I forget because I drank so much and used so many drugs or did drinking and using all the time make me forget all the stuff I needed to do? It's hard to say. A doctor, whose name I naturally cannot remember, once told me that the amount of ecstasy I used alone probably had some long term effect on my memory. Thus I'm inclined to think it's a little bit of both for. I drank for the specific purpose of forgetting and under some delusional guise that things would take care of themselves. Also, the amount I used most likely caused some form of chemical induced amnesia. I remember being in an appointment with a psychiatrist and peeking at his clipboard. Under the list of ailments and things he was looking for after hearing about my drug and alcohol use was "alcoholic dementia". Given my ability to forget everything, I was convinced that is what I had. Turns out it wasn't. Regardless of what caused my forgetting, it was a jacked up combination when it comes to remembering to take care of your basic needs, your body and your teeth.

After days of torture, I wound up at a dentist's office down the street from our house in Denver. "It's like if Melrose Place was in the future at a dentist's office," I told my husband. My dentist was a blond woman actually named Dr. Glamm and every dental hygienist looked like they stepped off of a Men's Health cover. It was impossibly clean and had that sleek over-the-top late 2000's design that people will see in ten years and laugh uncontrollably at. However, they were really nice and more than that, they didn't judge my ass for the shoddy shape of my grill. Doctor Glamm made sure

I was comfortable and walked me through the whole process. Telling me all the gross things going on with my teeth and how they'd help the pain go away, she left no stone unturned. With a name like Glamm, I'm sure being sciencey and thorough is a necessary cross to bear. After the consultation, they decided my teeth would have to go which was fine by me. After yanking three angry teeth from my mouth, I was more swollen and out of it then when I came in but already feeling better. They tried really hard to make sure I left with a Vicodin prescription and finally I had to tell Dr. Glamm to chill out. I told her I would try to tough it out on Advil, but I'd let her know. "I can just write you the prescription and you can hang onto it if you need it," she said. Pills weren't even my gig, but I wasn't in the mood to make them my gig so again, I declined her offer. Later, I was fit for partials and sent on a path to now take better care of my teeth.

As I write this some six years later, I am reminded that I need to go back to the dentist, the eye doctor, a general physician, and I need to reach out the company in charge of my student loans. Alas, all of those things I forgot to do didn't go anywhere and didn't vanish on their own. Most of them followed suit of my teeth, meaning they got worse. A few relationships, few dings on my credit and more than a few health concerns got downright bad. Just because I forgot to handle them doesn't mean they stayed frozen in time. They wiggled, they wrestled, they swelled up, and they festered. Some even exploded. The to-do list grows and morphs into more of a to-do rabbit hole. Oddly enough, however, these things I forgot were all pretty patient.

They let me get to them when I could. While they had mainly gotten worse, like my teeth, they got knocked off my list one way or another. Unable to make a dent in the aforementioned student loans, the government swiped some of my income tax return to help me out. Aww, thanks government. While I would have liked to spend that money on shoes or a trip to Mexico, it was at least more "handled" than it was before. It also provided a push to take care of some credit stuff that I wouldn't have done on my own because you know I'm still secretly holding out for magic to take care of all of my problems. Why work on becoming more productive when you can still hold out for magic? Sure I could empty the cat's litter box, but so could an enchanted band of merry litter box elves! Why wouldn't I wait for that?

All of this leads me to the bigger "issue" simmering underneath the things I forgot to do; I'm maybe not much of a motivated doer on my own. Which is to say, maybe I need a push from the government or for my refrigerator to stink really badly or for my teeth to rot out of my face before I do something and maybe that's okay. Sure, it would be great if I was super fucking organized and was able to handle all my stuff in an afternoon. The fact of the matter is, Chelsea, I'm not much of a handler. I'm more of a doer or go getter, but only when it's absolutely necessary or if I'm in enough pain. That's definitely what happened with my teeth and like a billion times the case when it came to getting sober, but neither one of those things turned out that bad. Eventually.

Cool Intentions

AT ONE POINT in the music video, the singer, whom we'd really only seen in close up, starts to dance. She doesn't dance in a Janet Jackson carefully choreographed way, but more like a subtle shimmy wherein she tosses her head back and forth. It's all so effortless but looks so fantastic that we don't question it nor do we want more from her as a dancer. At no point in this music video do you find yourself ever saying, "Gee. They could have given us a little something extra. Some backup dancers. A storyline. Something." This is remarkable because the video really only consists of the aforementioned singer and the rest of the band performing their catchy, now iconic song. Somehow all of it is enough, more than enough in fact. When we first see her, it's a tight close up. She's lip syncing, but not in that late 70's early 80's way that was either overly dramatic or hilariously awkward. She's lip syncing like she's this incredibly unimpressed yet approachable chick just telling us a story. With shimmery eye shadow, legendary tousled blonde hair with dark highlights and lips covered in a lip gloss so shiny you can almost see your reflection in them, she's certainly a beauty but there's more to her than that. She's really fucking cool. She's so cool that people for decades will still be trying to Xerox her brand of magic and never get close. She's Debbie Harry and she's the person who made me think as a small child, "That's what I want to be. I want to be cool!"

That 1979 video for Heart of Glass is sort of the impossible gold standard for me when it comes to cool. This is hilarious because there's not really too much to it. Just Debbie and the boys from Blondie rocking out in a dingy New York nightclub. Sure, the guys are wearing impeccable striped t shirts that any modern Brooklynite would die for and visually it presents this eye catching glimpse at a New York that no longer exists. It's not Thriller or some other big storytelling music extravaganza. It's just some artsy kids and their band playing a catchy hit. It's simple and that's what maybe makes it so cool. To me, cool and effortless always went hand and hand. Being cool means looking great and presenting yourself in a way that felt seamless. Debbie Harry didn't try to be cool. She just was. Making it a hard thing to pin down and obtain. Being athletic or even being well liked as a kid had certain checkpoints and tasks that could help you get closer to your silly little social goal, but being cool was more of a state of mind. Sure, you needed the right wardrobe but that wouldn't cut it alone if you still acted like a dork or listened to the wrong music or hung out with non-cool people. In my mind, it was a total lifestyle commitment and a hard one to pull off, especially when you were a scrawny effeminate kid like me who played with dolls until he was 13.

I certainly gave it my best shot however, and thankfully a really great taste in music helped at least present a surface illusion that I knew about cool stuff. Therefore, I must be cool, right? My older sister gifted me and my brothers with knowledge of the bands to like and not like. It was up to us to use that knowledge wisely to win cool friends. Cool music, cool clothes and stupid looking but cool 80's haircuts did the deal at age 12 and 13, but as I got older and felt internally more horrible about myself, it wasn't enough. Finding cool kids that drank, smoked and did drugs put it in another stratosphere. Being an addict from the jump meant that adding substances to my pursuit of being cool now had a buffer and a mission statement. I was in search of cool and getting fucked up. Again, all well and good for teens and twenty somethings and sort of expected.

But hanging onto this idea of chasing cool even when you're not drinking and well into your forties? Yeesh.

I realized I was still hooked on cool over the past year. I moved to a new town due to Michael's, job. It was like I was 13 again, in a position where I needed new friends. Thankfully, the rooms of recovery are filled with people who have what I have and who are always down to hang out and have coffee. By the nature of being badass survivors, all of whom have some gnarly tales to tell, most of these folks are what I would consider cool. So, I wasn't worried about them being cool; it was me. The meetings were like going back to my junior high days; I found myself going for people who I considered to be cool, hoping they would say hi or laugh at what I shared. I don't smoke anymore, but don't think I didn't consider picking it back up to perhaps win a bunch of new cool friends. However, we moved to Portland where a lot of sober people vape. Not even if the ghost of 1950's Marlon Brando came back to this realm in a leather jacket to vape with Debbie Harry herself, would it ever make me think vaping was cool. Instead of vaping, what followed was a series of stilted conversation and goofy attempts to relate to people.

Making friends as an old person is hard, y'all. Graciously, the universe and the internet provided me with a fabulous friend when I moved here. We had met on Twitter and thankfully liked each other in person. She showed me the ropes, in and outside of the rooms and is a writer to boot. Others followed and soon I found myself surrounded by people I really liked and not whom I hunted down and took hostage because of their perceived coolness. We spoke the same language, we made each other laugh and we leaned on one another. It was effortless actually and in turn very cool. Watching that Blondie video now, almost 40 years later, it's still really cool. But it's kind of dorky too. Like Debbie and her bandmates don't really give a crap if they look like weirdos or act a fool. They've got great outfits on but seem pretty nerdy at heart. When one band member checks his hair in a spinning disco ball, this isn't a Fonzie type move but reads more like a tongue in cheek joke to being cool itself. The members of Blondie look like they don't give a fuck. It's precisely this, the not caring what people think part of being cool, that I was actually chasing for all those years. I desperately wanted to not care if I was wearing the right thing or if I said the right thing or if some random person that seemed like sort of a dick anyway thought I was cool. When I slide back there today, however, I know what it's about. It's about chasing ideals that don't exist.

The truth is, my idea of cool now has changed. People who go to bed early are cool. People who are nice for no real reason are cool. Mainly, people who genuinely don't care what I think because they've done a lot of work to get to that place, thank you very much, are cool. On my best days, I'm one of those people too.

Angry Anymore

BUBBLE. Furiously simmer. Boil over. Explode. Repeat for 10 to 20 years. This was the family recipe passed on for generations of hotheaded alcoholics. I'd seen this dish prepared and served my whole life. The chefs in charge were not to be messed with. Once they started making it, you got out of the way. The funny thing is, I never thought I was one of them. You know, one of those angry yelling types who blew the fuck up out of nowhere and for no good reason. Those assholes were cray-cray. I mean, I loved them and I was related to them but they needed to relax. I also thought that I wasn't an alcoholic, so what did I know?

Turns out, your buddy ole smiling Sean Mahoney is one angry muthafucker. I was able to learn this through a series of writings; the kids in programs that help people stop killing themselves with drugs and alcohol, call it "stepwork." The more I wrote and looked at my past actions, the more I realized how incredibly pissed off I was. I was pissed off at Catholic school teachers who humiliated me, pissed off at exes who didn't love me enough, and pissed off at myself for making the same mistakes year after year. If I looked at this stuff and found my part and cleaned up my messes, I'd feel better and maybe, just maybe I'd stop drinking to dull how angry I was. They turned out to be right. Seven years later, they are still right. I'm back into doing this kind of writing again and I guess I should explain why. A mutual friend with the same time as me relapsed, couldn't stop and killed himself. Another friend who I got sober with in 2009 and with more time than me went out and now struggles to stay sober. And yet another beloved friend had seven years but relapsed and has spent the last seven trying to get sober. He just celebrated a year. This sort of thing happens in recovery a lot but for some reason these events got to me this year. All of these people had the amount of time I had and suddenly did not. I was terrified. So I asked my sponsor if we could do the work again. Thus, here I am looking at how angry I am yet again.

There was also something else. Something I really didn't want to look straight in the face and actually own. I had gotten really angry in sobriety a few times and it felt crushing. Here was a behavior that I knew could kill me. I had the receipts on how it's ruined the lives of people in my family, yet I've somehow defaulted to it, more than I wanted to admit. One incident in particular stands out.

I was on the board of a theatre company with my husband. I handled the publicity for the company and managed to get in a few local magazines. In an interview, I made a joke about Mitt Romney being like Marie Antoinette. I stand by it as a good joke but will reluctantly admit that maybe a fluffy PR interview wasn't the place for a political joke. No, fuck that.

Theatre is political and the joke was solid so I ain't admitting shit. Clearly, I still have a lot of work to do. Anyway, this joke went over like a lead balloon with the uptight, conservative blonde who was the head of our board. She wanted to talk about it and I was already incensed. Walking in with guns blazing, it was less of a conversation and more of a fingers wagging in the face, Real Housewives sort of showdown. There was no wig pulling or table flipping, but trust that my inner Nene Leakes and Teresa Giudice were raging. It lasted all of ten minutes, but supremely fucked me up for days. I bolted from that meeting and immediately wound up in the other kind of meetings I routinely go to. I was devastated that in a blink of an eye I could hop right back into crazy, angry bitch behavior. It felt like a fail. It felt like I should know better. Most terrifying though, it felt like something I could drink over.

I realize for me, like the generations of hothead Irish alcoholics before me, that anger is poison. I've had two maybe three big, angry explosions in sobriety. They feel awful. They feel out of control. They feel like the kind of thing that would make me go back to drinking. Rage is equally as deadly as drugs and alcohol and I've seen people destroyed by it. Therefore, I have to look at it. I have to treat it. I have to write about it. Sigh. Seven years later, I'm still wishing for the unsavory parts of my character to vanish but they don't unless I do a little work on them. This time around, I'm discovering there's still a few things that I'm really angry about. It's deeper, less superficial stuff though. I'm angry at America. I'm at angry at the news. I'm angry at the way we treat each other. I'm angry at racist, homophobic, sexist, intolerant assholes, in general. But the people I dated, the people who raised me, the people I drank with and probably pissed off too? Child. No. I've prayed for those hoes and released them.

The other part of this, is the tricky part. Making a conscious decision to not choose anger.

Miraculously, through doing this stuff that seems impossible and like a real pain in the neck, things I thought I'd never get over, I'm just not angry about anymore. Really. There's a lot of forgiveness. There's even more accountability. There's a strong recognition that being crazy and angry for me is a toxic place to be. On my best days, I can let anger say its thing and explode and then tell it, "Thank you for sharing. Now, go sit your angry ass down." On my worst days? I try to

shut up and not hurt people.

My sponsor told me to look at the people and things I

resent and realize which ones have to do with

acceptance. Who am I unwilling to accept the way they

are? Turns out, that's almost everyone. For me, I can be

sad today. I can have compassion. I can even be

disappointed by the world and the people who

populate it. I can also take action and change the things

I'm mad about. I just can't be angry anymore.

Nobody Gives a Fuck
How You Stay Sober

I SAY THIS from a place of love, light and spirituality: nobody gives a fuck. No, I'm serious and I swear once you wear this idea like a big old cozy sweater, the better off you will be. The pain of being convinced that people actually care and are overly invested in our every move is some 21st century narcissistic bullshit that serves no purpose other than to make you insane. This is especially true when we talk about getting sober. Everybody (and by everybody I mean addicts because, let's be honest, we are some selfish ass bitches and we think we are everybody) is convinced that how they are trying to get sober is constantly being scrutinized or judged. We think we're doing it wrong. We think that we found a way to stay sober and it needs to be shouted out from the rafters. Baby, I'm here to tell you, ain't nobody give a fuck.

The most boring thing on the internet today is the blog post deep-fried in clickbait batter that says, "Why AA Sucks!" or conversely "Why AA is the only way to get sober." If you have clicked on either one of these types of article, you've been played, sucka. The people who write these things don't want to honestly connect with other people struggling with addiction. They want to scream about how right they are into a void. That's as boring to me as the billions of angry comments left on these posts. It's all inflammatory BS concocted to get page views and not substance. My mom always says, "Hurt people hurt other people," but hurt people also write attention seeking blog posts and it's all nonsense. Bo to the ring.

I find it so brain-splatteringly boring for a few reasons. First of all, people struggling to stay sober need to cling onto whatever life raft they find and your anti 12-Step program posts aren't helping. If somebody about to die, finds comfort there and stays sober, leave them the fuck alone. Likewise, if 12 step programs aren't somebody's thing, don't beat the fuck out of them. It's attraction rather than promotion, my AA homie, and you should know better. Stop yelling in all caps quotes from the big book. We've ceased fighting, dawg, and you should know that too. Also, I find it boring because these arguments back and forth deflate the real issue at hand: THAT PEOPLE ARE DYING, YOU SELFISH TURD AND YOUR OPINIONS AREN'T HELPING ANYONE , he ironically yells in all caps. Seriously if we all spent as much time waxing poetically on the best ways to stay sober as we did actually helping struggling addicts and alcoholics in real life, we'd be better off. Lastly, I think it's boring because it solves nothing. I'm a cocaine addict, mind you, so I like some instant ass results. Okay, fight back and forth, but let's have something useful come out of these conversations. Otherwise, I cannot be bothered.

I got sober through AA primarily because I'm uncreative and I was out of options. Relying on just smoking weed, hiding from alcohol or good old-fashioned magic to keep me sober didn't work. I sincerely hope somebody out there tried one or more of those things and it helped you get sober. Particularly magic. Please, if magic made you sober, you owe the world a book and I will buy it. However, none of that shit worked for me and I did what family members and a billion friends did: I went to a ton of meetings. I didn't buy the whole AA kit and caboodle at first and guess what - nobody gave a fuck. These were a bunch of screwed up people like me. Sure, they wanted to help if they could but honey child, they were hot messes too, so they did what they could. But nobody was too worried about if I was "feeling it" or if I needed to be converted. I either got on board or I didn't. These folks were just trying not to die. I could do what they were doing and if not, that's cool too.

After a while, it all sort of clicked. Yet as I have mentioned numerous times, it was not all good in the formerly drunken hood. In fact, it was all jacked up for a long ass time, but I was desperate not to be the same drunken a-hole I had been for 20 plus years, so I did whatever people said worked for them. AA saved my life, but mainly because I did ALL of the shit they tell you to do and all of the 12 Steps. Weird that we'd even have to point out that a 12 Step program only works if you do the entire thing, but you'd be surprised at how many people went to two meetings, never opened their mouths or did a step and then declared, "AA is some bullshit!" That'd be like hating on Paris even though you had only flown over it and never actually walked around the damn place. Anyway, AA did what it was supposed to do for me and has kept me sober for nearly 10 years. I never felt bullied or pressured or shamed by people in AA. Annoyed, exhausted and irritated by people in AA, yes, but to be fair, that's how I feel about most people everywhere.

Still, I recognize the spirituality part is a tough pill to swallow for people and that it isn't everybody's jam. Lots of folks stay sober through church, even more stay sober through yoga, and some with just the support of loved ones. Refuge Recovery. SMART Recovery. Celebrate Recovery. CrossFit. Therapy. Biking. Knitting. Whatever it takes. I say anything that keeps us off the streets and stops us from being drunk, drugged out terrors at places like Target or the airport, then I'm all about it. Acting like I'm some authority or expert on staying sober or that my way is the only way is stupid. Likewise, so is beating up people for staying sober through ways I don't understand. Listen, it still takes a lot to get my own sober behind out of bed and out the door. I don't have time to micromanage your program of recovery. You found it, whatever it is that keeps you sober and I'm truly happy for you! Please keep doing what you're doing and please help some damn people find the sober juju you have found!

After about 18 months without drinking, I walked into my old grocery store in Echo Park. The cashier was a girl named Roxy who rang me up dozens of times and definitely saw me totally shit housed more than a few times. "Did you need a bottle today," she asked. I told her I didn't and that I hadn't drunk in over a year. "Oh thank God," she said. "You were really bad." You're a special kind of neighborhood alcoholic when even the girl at the grocery store notices. She wasn't lying, though. I was no longer stumbling into the grocery store and everybody was happy about that, myself included.

The thing was Roxy didn't care how I stayed sober. She was just glad I did.

A Hot Mess,
Now at Room Temperature

You really need to get your shit together, they told me.

"They" were friends and family. "They" were

coworkers. "They" didn't exactly say it in so many

words as so much gently imply that perhaps maybe

there were better ways to conduct my life that didn't make me feel like a walking, smoking human dumpster. No, I was the one who said it to myself over and over again. "You really need to get your shit together" is pretty much the through line of mental thought I had for the last 5 years of my drinking and using. Let me tell you, that's a bummer of a message to play on repeat. Thankfully, drugs and alcohol make it go away very quickly. "You really need to get your shit together." Oh yeah? Let me pour tequila and cocaine on you until you shut up.

See, nobody ever wants to hear that their shit isn't together. Nobody wants to be told, even by themselves, that they are a disaster. We all live a delusion on some level that we are absolutely nailing this whole life thing. Besides, compared to someone like a serial killer or somebody living with kittens under a bridge, my shit was together. So what if I couldn't pay my bills and was hung over 7 days a week? At least, I wasn't wanted by the law or trying to hide a body. These are admittedly low bars to set for the whole "getting your shit together" thing. Alas, with that message playing for so long and things getting progressively worse, I had to "get my shit together." Eight and a half years later, my shit is together. But is it really?

By telling my story and writing about being an addict and alcoholic, I've landed in a magical yet bizarre place. I am incredibly lucky to get to write about my past and my recovery. Each time I do, I feel the burden of my old life loosen and it all gets progressively more ridiculous and funnier as time goes on. It is indisputably a gift and I cherish being connected to so many other writers in recovery who day after day share their story of getting better. For me, writing about this stuff is therapeutic and if somebody else happens to get something out of it, fantastic. I think of it as a way of being of service, so I try not to get fucked up about comments and page views and collective digital approval, which is a drug in its own right. We, who write about this sort of stuff, are part of a community which is truly amazing. This community has spilled into my real life and lifted me up in the most unexpected ways.

Yet, it ain't perfect. I don't share many of the popular recovery stories out there. I'm not a high bottom drunk. I don't hate calling myself an addict (please do not get me started on that). I don't do inspirational memes or go on yoga retreats. All of those things are fine but that's not my sobriety. I'm also not straight (spoiler alert lol) so I'm kind of the lone gay, pink wolf in this pack which is actually fantastic as lord knows Miss Thing likes being unique. The other thing? I'm not a sobriety expert or sober coach or life coach or life fixer. God no, I'd be terrible at that. I am simply an experience sharer, which all brings me back to the title. Sometimes, most of the time, the experience is that I'm still a mess and far from being some sort of mental health icon. Eight years in, I really wish I could tell you I never acted like an addict ever again and all of my character defects disappeared in a poof of lavender glitter. Likewise, I wish I could tell you my self-esteem is rock solid and I'm just insanely in love with myself. Sadly, I cannot.

After shopping for new clothes, eating a delicious meal and having time with friends, I still felt empty. That old hole in myself that needs to be filled but given its endless nature can never be, popped back up. I wanted something, anything to fix me. Today I know the truth about that hole. No amount of Netflix or chocolate or dick or drugs or alcohol can fill it. I should have laid down or reached out or went to a meeting, but instead I just drove myself nuts for a while until I got tired and went to bed. The following day, I woke up with an emotional hangover. I prayed, I meditated, I ate a great breakfast and I vowed to be nicer to myself. Lo and behold, I was nicer to myself and I felt better. I woke up today happy and well rested. I realize that this is all a moment-by-moment proposition all contingent on how I take care of myself.

It's also why I can't be a sobriety or mental health guru. I'm just some idiot who was fortunate to get help from other addicts and alcoholics and managed to stay sober, one muthafucking day at a time. I no longer drink when life gets hard or annoying (and it does frequently). I have tools I can use and will begrudgingly do so when I'm in enough pain. That being said, there's a pathway to a happier Sean that even if I follow to the letter doesn't ensure total daily bliss. Even with money in my bank account, a roof over my head and years of sobriety under my belt, my shit isn't necessarily together. I am still a hot mess but now I'm served at room temp.

PART II

SWIM TOWARD
THE LIGHT

I'm a spiritual being, muthafuckers

LET'S GET THIS out of the way before we roll up our sleeves and really talk about God: people who wear "Spiritual gangsta" hoodies, refer to themselves as gurus or have things like "Christ first" in their Twitter bios are the worst. I mean, I get it. Everyone is seeking something, so maybe these folks need to fly their freaky spirituality flag to let the world know how down with G.O.D. they really are. Still, it does feel obnoxious. The most spiritual and God-like people I ever met were the ones who were humble and did amazing acts for their fellow-man on the DL They didn't need sweatshirts or Facebook groups to prove that they had spiritual lives. But who am I to judge really? I'm a seeker like everyone else, even the spiritual gangsta. And this whole road of seeking is, as far as I can tell, a messy affair.

I don't really do organized religion. I'm not much of joiner, I find religious services to be snoozy and oh yeah, I sort of hate people. These things don't really make yours truly the ideal candidate to organize your church picnic. Therefore I am not Catholic or Christian or Buddhist. I never felt like I had to pick a tribe to join in order to have a god, as weird as that sounds. Nevertheless, I have a version of God and spiritual life. Go figure. I had long thought the two went hand in hand and you couldn't have one without the other. But, much like chocolate and peanut butter, I've discovered some people can enjoy religion and spirituality together while others have them a la carte. Thanks to getting sober, I found God. Not like God was missing; He's not Carmen Sandiego or something. I wasn't struck by a lightning bolt and didn't start dancing in the streets and speaking in tongues. I simply found something bigger than myself. My own version of God has a sense of humor (obvi) and takes its own damn time figuring things out but is always there for me. That's really all I can tell because it's my God, not yours.

I'm a middle child and bad at sharing. Get your own damn God, god dammit.

This thing bigger than me and more powerful than me keeps expanding and I'm still desperately seeking God. This apparently is good news. I was in a Saturday morning meeting with drunks and drugs addicts, as I've been known to do, and there was a woman celebrating 30 years sober. She talked about moving through rough patches recently. She shared honestly about not always feeling connected to her version of God. But mainly, what I heard, was a woman who was sharing about still seeking. She's still looking to strengthen the spiritual connection, to grow and to keep changing and getting better. By sharing about struggling, but somehow persisting and staying sober anyway, she let me and presumably the others in the packed room know that we were okay just where we are. Because God and from what I can tell spirituality in general isn't some graduate program or reality tv competition. There isn't an end in sight or a certificate to achieve.

God is on my mind recently because I noticed I had several conversations about God with recently. As an old AA friend of mine once said, sober people either talk about alcohol or they talk about God and , it was primarily the latter. Life is a mystery, as my own spiritual conduit Madonna once said, and therefore so is God. When I have conversations about God with sober people, that's sort of what we're doing: unravelling the mystery and getting clues from one another on how you do this whole god thing. Before I stopped drinking and using drugs, I thought God was some punishing being who hated me for being gay and was probably still low-key pissed off at what a bad Catholic I was. So, I need to see and hear what God is for other people and then go off continue to seek my own.

Therefore it isn't really my business if someone has a God who hates gay people or belongs to a religion that oppresses women. Likewise, it's not my concern if Facebook friends post overly religious crap. I'm too busy trying not to be a horrible person, one day at time. I guess even the guy in the "Spiritual Gangsta" hoodie gets a pass. That said, I'm gonna hold off on ordering one for myself.

Private Chanter

IF I HAVE unrealistic expectations, don't blame me; blame Tina Turner. Witnessing Tina Turner live and onstage at age 12 has forever warped my expectations of what mere mortals should be able to do. I thought that every woman could dance and run around for 90 minutes in seven inch high heels (they cannot). I thought that every person in their 50's looked and acted like her (they do not). Much to my dismay, I also thought that every soul diva to come after her would be just as excellent and as we know they are not. In fact, I really blame Tina Turner for me not loving Beyoncé. Had I never seen Tina Turner live and experienced her funky rock and roll voodoo in person maybe, I'd be more impressed with Beyoncé. Alas, I did see her on tour (with Stevie Wonder no less!) and therefore I am decidedly not. This is not Beyoncé's fault. I am just wired differently because of this experience. Having not seen many live performances at that age, I still knew on a cellular level that this firestorm of a person was incredible. Every song, every dance move, every interaction with the audience was a masterclass on how rock and roll should be done. On a spiritual level,

I think I needed this cosmic interaction with Tina Turner as a 12-year-old. Maybe her resilience and survival were subconsciously telling me to hang in there or maybe she was just incredibly fierce and ran around non-stop in leather.

Either way, my expectations were high and made even higher when I saw What's Love Got To Do With It? in theaters in 1993. Please watch this immediately to properly find your way to the Church of Tina Turner. Anchored by two of the best performances of the 1990s, courtesy of Angela Bassett and Laurence Fishburn, the film tells Tina's life story and her escape from her abusive marriage to Ike Turner. It's a phenomenal film made even better by the packed house of primarily black women where I saw it on opening weekend. The scene in the limo where Tina finally leaves is powerful on its own, but gets rocketed into a whole other dimension of amazing when the audience is hollering at the screen, "That's right, girl! Leave his ass!" Yet, the scene that really stuck with me was when Tina gets introduced to Buddhism by one of the Ikettes. She is shown chanting, "nam myoho renge kyo." I was almost 21 when I saw that movie and seeking something else. By then, I'd already done enough ecstasy that it stopped working and moved my car over into the meth lane with disastrous results. Unexplainably, these three minutes of spirituality on film were powerful for some reason.

Flash forward to the summer of 2009. I had moved from the East side to the West Side in Los Angeles, which is a cultural faux pas akin to leaving the Democratic Party to become a Republican. But I did it to get sober. Thankfully, my roommate at the time was also sober and practicing Daishonin Buddhism. The religion, as it turns out, is primarily based on chanting "nam myoho renge kyo." When she asked if I was familiar, I of course acted like an expert. But the reality was all I knew of nam myoho renge kyo was the three minutes from the movie. Still, it worked for Tina Turner and it looked like it was working for my roommate and her friends so I thought I'd give it a try. She taught me how to chant at home, took me to Buddhist events and I started to read more about it. Listen, I was in bad shape after 20 years of drugs and alcohol and I was pretty much open to anything. It felt good when I chanted and it didn't seem like it could hurt. The idea to go get tested for HIV came to me while chanting. It had been years and it was way past due.

Chanting also brought up strong and difficult emotions about the past. When I got my positive diagnosis and other parts of my life started to fall apart, I realized that maybe I was a tad out of depth with this chanting thing. Maybe my Tina Turner expectations around my newfound spirituality were unrealistic too?

Like a good drug addict, I wanted all of my recovery and spirituality to work fast and make me instantly feel better. So when chanting brought up difficult stuff, it scared the hell out of me. At the time, I felt like I unleashed a whirlwind with this spiritual tool and I was freaked out. Pretty quickly, I dropped chanting as a practice. However, the reality was my life was fucked up thanks to the damage I did. Chanting simply brought it all to the surface. The shit was destined to hit the fan (and continue to do so for several months) and chanting just expedited it. Also, those three minutes in the movie, although powerful, don't tell the whole story. Any good Tina fan knows that her battles with Ike and struggles to get her career back were just beginning, so chanting was just a practice and not some cure-all for her either. She continued chanting and her life, as we know, gradually improved.

Even though I stopped chanting, my life improved too. Feeling like I fast tracked a religious life too quickly, I just went to meetings and tried to keep my life simple. It was going to take a lot of time to get honest, to change my thinking and to stop feeling horrible. My spiritual life was stripped down to the basics. Prayers in the morning and at night and that was it. That's all my little drug damaged head could handle. I introduced more meditation at a year and a half sober, but I naturally did that alcoholically too at 30 minutes a day and was forced to make that easier as well.

This morning, I meditated while the sun came up for ten minutes as the cats took turns walking across my lap. I giggled at them and took sips of coffee and gently pushed my thoughts back to meditation. I'm not exactly levitating these days or being sought after for spiritual advice, but my prayer and meditation feels honest, which is huge for a lying addict like me. What's more is the thing I really loved about Tina Turner, her spirit of survival and ability to come out the other side of horrific times, is something I get to see in real life when I hang out every day with other sober addicts and alcoholics. I even get to see it in myself and I don't have to wear leather or high heels, but I might anyway.

BUT I'M ALREADY SO TIRED

IF WE HANG out together more than once, you'll undoubtedly hear me sigh, "My phone's about to die." If I work all day, "my phone's about to die." If you're about to launch into a really good story, "my phones about to die." How have you been? "My phone's about to die." What's my go-to order at Popeye's? "My phone's about to die." It's not personal. It's just now at the every fabric of who I am. Due to obsessive

128

compulsive tweeting, general forgetfulness and a blissful laissez faire that can't be bothered to learn how to run fewer apps, my phone is always on the brink of near death. It's so perpetually in low power mode, I often wonder if there's a setting that can just alert me when it is actually charged instead of wasting its breath to always tell me that my phone's days are numbered. Yet as with those phony tweets announcing Betty White's death, my phone is alive and well. Just in a perpetual state of low energy. My phone battery, myself. Neither me nor my phone is actually about to die, but we're usually not running on full power.

Being gifted with an immune system that behaves like a dainty Southern belle who fans herself while her suitors fetch her lemonades means my baseline is just sort of exhausted. Not exhausted in a way that actually dying people with hardcore active illnesses are, but in a way that I'm certainly not going to hustle just to prove that I can. Much like that phone battery, I've got to conserve my energy. When it comes to HIV and the meds they give you to handle it, exhaustion is a puzzle. Is it the HIV that makes you exhausted, is it the meds, or is it the still stupid societal prejudice and misunderstanding of the disease that makes us positive people exhausted? Who knows and I'm too tired to even Google any of this. Truthfully, it's probably all of those things, but what I know is that I'm not the only tired bitch with HIV roaming the Earth. This is comforting. We the people with teeny tiny immune systems march forward with coffees in hand and we're too tired to put up with your bullshit. This right here is the ultimate gift of being tired all the time.

Tired All The Time is the sequel to Eddie Murphy's hit song *Party All The Time* but he was too tired to release it.

When you have a smaller bandwidth, you have to be selective about the things you let ruffle your feathers. Admittedly, in an era with overt racism, constant nuclear threat, sexual predators in positions of power and every known system collapsing, ruffling feathers seems like a delicate way to put it. Feathers ruffled feels like something we could easily get over. Most of this shit? I'm not too sure about that. More accurately described as "a world in decline," as per my talisman in black eyeliner, Chrissie Hynde, society today could really flatten you if you let it all get to you. Therefore, I'm grateful that my rage, disgust and depression has to be selective. It's express lane outrage, 9 items or less.

The reality for me is that a lot of it is going to bother me and get me down. Congratulations to those folks who tell you any chance they get that they've stopped reading everything, their lives are so much better and that you should really try it. I'm happy for them, but I am not them. The world bugs me and that feels healthy for me. After all, what would I write about if I didn't sort of low key hate everyone/everything? So I pick and choose what to angry about. Likewise, I get to pick who and what I put energy into.

I recently spent a lot of time chasing someone. Not romantically, mind you and certainly not literally as in running, dear God, no. I was trying to get a friend to hang out with me, to spend time with me, hell to even call me back. It was an exhausting place to be. Seriously, what the fuck was I doing? I'm already so tired and now I'm spending time running after a friend who clearly doesn't want to spend time with me? Girl. What is this, seventh grade? I eventually released this friend without a bunch of conversations or drama (shit I'm really way too tired to do). One sided relationships of any kind fall firmly into the "I'm too tired for this shit" folder and I have to remember to keep them there. Also in that folder:

* People who dominate conversations

* Late people

* Flaky people

*Standing in line for lame events

*Entitled people

*Arguing with people

*People. Kidding. Sort of.

Writing this list, it doesn't escape me that most of these things that make me more tired are things that I myself am guilty of. Whomp, whomp. Naturally, the bullshit that I am the most sick of and that makes me the most tired is my own. Oh, self-awareness, way to fuck things up once again. Nevertheless, it's true. I am very tired of my own flakiness, my own entitlement, my impulse to argue with people even when I know better. While the president, the people of planet earth and basically any time I have to go to a store like Home Depot can make me exhausted, it's my own stuff that really gets tiresome.

Of course, it's also the stuff that's easiest to change. Like, Sean, maybe don't argue? Maybe don't open your mouth for five minutes? Maybe let someone go ahead of you in line? While my phone is currently at 53%, my energy is considerably less than that, yet I'm actually okay. Maybe running on half a battery provides me the reflection that I can be less horrible and conserve personal energy. It certainly can't hurt. I can take the focus of my own exhaustion and try to meditate on being some sort of flawed spiritual being whom at the very least doesn't make other people tired. But first, I need to take a nap.

DEATH STRAIGHT UP

The musical prophet, Jennifer Love Hewitt, once posed the question, "How do I deal?" I apologize for the random reference, but I have a mental glitch which forces me to remember every terrible song ever released by a television star. I also have alcoholism which means, sorry J-Love, when it comes to "dealing," my strategy is simple: I don't.

I've spent my 40-something years on the planet trying my damnedest to avoid life's unsavory moments. For example, I once got in a car accident and then immediately took a nap instead of dealing with the literal wreckage right in front of me. Normally, I would just take handfuls of drugs and buckets of booze to obliterate reality. For years, I tried to drink away the death of my favorite grandfather who died in 1997. Then, when I got sober in 2009, his death (and a mountain of other things) were still there and they still hurt like hell. When his wife, my grandmother, died last month, I had to do the unthinkable: I had to deal.

After 15 years in Los Angeles, where I bottomed out and then got sober, I left and found myself living in the Denver neighborhood where I grew up. Thanks to extensive exorcisms on my past, I'd gotten over my childhood stuff. Not because I'm some emotionally evolved guru, but because I needed to if I wanted to figure out why my life was a booze drenched disaster. The bonus of living here in 2016 is getting to see my childhood with fresh eyes and with an acceptance I never thought possible. Another bonus? My grandmother lived right up the street.

This ninja-level organizer who had eight children, ten rotating weekly social commitments and dozens of friends was a saving grace when I was growing up a block away in an alcoholic home. Sensing everything wasn't okay on the ranch, she and my grandfather often took me and my siblings on trips to the mountains, to McDonalds for Happy Meals or to look at Christmas lights. Their mission was one filled with seemingly simple gestures aimed to reinforce the idea that our lives might be crazy but we were always loved. Now sober and middle-aged, I welcomed the opportunity to hang out with my grandmother and help her with simple stuff: checking emails, transcribing her writings and anything digital that might be exhausting for an 89-year-old. I was in no way trying to be a saint or win some kind of "Greatest Grandkid" award. I just considered it a tiny way to repay for her all that she'd done. Plus, she was hilarious and I liked spending time with her.

Over the last year, I watched her become increasingly frail. I had more than one tear-filled conversation with my husband about how I thought our time with Grandma was ticking away. When she died on October 8th, I entered uncharted territory as a grown up, sober person without the cocaine and tequila force-field to protect me from death and all of the crazy ass stuff it brings with it.

Weird. That's the only word I can describe death. Sorry, I'm not freaking Elisabeth Kübler-Ross but "weird" really covers the whole experience. The act of dying itself is weird. She had this very lovely farewell where she got to say goodbye in her home for a week before checking out of the hotel permanently, but the whole thing was surreal and—yes—weird. People were popping in at all hours to say goodbye to Grandma, but to also tell me about some obscure story from my childhood or to explain how they knew her and my massive Catholic family. The weirdness just trickled down. Getting somebody to pick up the body? Weird. The random stuff people bring over to eat? Weird. My nights of erratic sleep filled with dreams about ghosts? Weird. The conversations you have with neighbors about your grandmother dying? Weird and sometimes funny, like the one I had with my 90-year old landlord, who has known my grandmother since the 1980s. He's a sweet man who is incredibly hard of hearing, so our conversations usually consist of what can best be described as friendly yelling. He called me after she'd been on her deathbed for several days. "Your grandmother is dying!" he shouted. "Yes. I know. Thanks for calling," I shouted back. My husband and I laughed at how horrible it would have been if this was actually how the news was broken to me.

The weirdness was compacted by the fact that I was present for all of it. Somehow, I rolled with every one of the weird, touching and WTF punches without picking up a drink. Still, I drank and used drugs for 20 years, so I'd be failing at this whole rigorous honesty thing if I said it didn't cross my mind. Look, "the obsession has been removed" as the kids say in meetings, but I'm also systematically to my core an addict. The reality is I'm going to think about drinking or doing drugs. Not all of the time (and now, not without playing the tape through on how disastrous it would be), but it's going to come up.

I took a walk outside a couple of days after she died and noticed empty wine bottles, clearly enjoyed by a family member of mine who didn't win the alcoholic lottery like I had. For two seconds, I sighed and thought, "Must be nice." Then, I remembered that me drinking wine was never nice or the classy, stemware on the French Riviera experience. My drinking was more of the two dollar Trader Joe's bottle on my porch under a veil of regret and bitterness variety. I also thought smoking looked pretty damned fantastic—to return to my chain-smoking, smack-talking Bette Davis roots in a time of personal despair seemed like a romantic notion. But I never wanted just one cigarette, I want to smoke all of them. Just go ahead and back that truck filled with Parliaments into the driveway and let me have at it. And just like that, the romance of being able to "take the edge off" with a few drinks or a couple of cigarettes disappears. Plus, this "edge" that we're all trying desperately to take off is kind of amazing.

Even though I knew she was dying, my heart was unequivocally broken. I had lost my neighbor, cheerleader, my grandmother and my friend who was desperately in love with my husband and thrilled that

I found sobriety. It was a kind of hurt I hadn't felt in my nearly eight years sober, and frankly, it sucked. I cried so much—and am not entirely out of the crying woods just yet. I kept texting sober friends and saying, "I don't know how I'm getting through this." To which they'd reply, "But you are" or "Honey, I'm praying for you." It was devastating and beautiful, too.

I'm broken, but I've also never felt as loved and supported as I have in the last few months. The thing about the weirdness, sadness and laughter is that all of it feels appropriate. It feels like I'm facing something difficult without chemicals to hide behind. It feels authentic. It feels like, for the first time in my life, I'm dealing with it.

Swim Toward the Light

WANDER AROUND ON a dark beach with two sweet ladies from West Texas long enough and you're bound to find something miraculous. That or you'll twist your ankle, whatever comes first. Nevertheless, that's what I found myself doing on Friday night. While most tourists were shaking their stuff at local nightclubs, the husband, the aforementioned Texans, myself and a guide were wandering around a Puerto Vallarta beach in the dark. The task at hand? Sea turtles. Baby ones, to be exact. The husband saw the "awwww!" look on my face when he mentioned a tour that worked with a sea turtle rescue and responded by booking said tour. From July to about December, big mama sea turtles pop up all over the shores of Puerto Vallarta, kind of like American tourists but better dressed. That guy I married and I often say to one another, "It'll be an adventure." This can apply to going into a really sketchy looking discount store or waiting in line at the post office or, in this case, helping sea turtles.

Now, I know what you're thinking: sea turtles who have been doing their thang on the shores of the planet for thousands of years certainly know what the hell they're doing, so why do they need people to help them? Thanks to our polluting and generally destructive asses, sea turtles are in trouble. So if we can make laying more eggs easier, protect those eggs and then help these little infants back into the ocean, we can hopefully grow the species as a whole. Therefore, we can reverse a teeny bit of the fuckery we've caused these poor creatures by ruining their oceans and hunting them.

Our five-person turtle-loving brigade walked along a stretch of beach populated by posh hotels and the obligatory white people who come along with them. Our mission? To see if we could find any mamas laying

148

eggs. The tour doesn't promise you'll see this phenomenon and wisely so. These mothers are on their own schedule and won't pop 'em out just so some family from Pomona can snap photos for their Instagram pages. But we optimistically trudged along the sand anyway. It was warm and quiet, the kind of beach quiet you can buy if you've got enough cash. I'm more of a hustle and bustle type so we were staying in a part of the city that actually looked like Mexico and less like glamour Burbank by the sea. After no sighting and with one of our Texas ladies exhaustedly taking solace under a tiki covered patio, we started to head back to the nursery. It wasn't going to be a complete wash. The rescue had set aside a bucket of flapping baby sea turtles that we could release when we returned.

As we walked, we ran into a 40-something Owen Wilson type and his equally blonde girlfriend crouched down in the sand with flashlights. The pair, along with some Solo cup clenching randoms, had stumbled on a hatching nest of baby sea turtles. Hundreds of them, as a matter of fact. Their ingenious but totally uninvolved mother buries the eggs by the dozens in the sand so when they hatch, they spring up, in the words of our guide, "like popcorn." And boy did they. The little guys kept crawling out of the sand, one by one. The minute you thought it had to be the end of this adorable family reunion, a bunch more would show up with sand covered heads and their itty bitty slits-for-eyes just barely opened. We'd pick them up and place them in the bucket. With their funny flapping arms and soft rubbery shells, I fell in love about 300 times that night as I placed them gently in this plastic waiting room before they went out into the world by themselves.

We were instructed not to use our flash as turtles use the light of the moon to guide them and a bunch of flashing lights could really disorient the little fellas. All on their own and without parents, these babies would learn to swim, eat and come back to shores like this one. It was all instinct and mystery and had nothing to do with me. What our group of five could do was help them out of the bucket. Turtle by turtle, we watched them flap, stumble and march towards the surf like little soldiers. In fact, they were off to quite the battle. Our guide informed us, because of predators, mainly shady birds which we saw earlier in the night nibbling on turtle eggs, only one in one hundred would survive. Our guide stood in the tide holding her flashlight acting as a beacon to hopefully direct turtle traffic into the water. "They'll swim towards the light," she said and gosh darn it, despite being only alive for a few moments they did precisely that. Waves rushed in and swooped some of them in the water. Others walked with purpose into the ocean. And a few more sort of meandered, taking their time and often required additional help getting near the water. I think we know which group I identified with.

As we wished them well on their journey, it struck me that really none of our odds are very good but somehow some of us make it. If you've beat cancer, you know what I'm talking about. If you've come back from the brink of mental illness, you know what I'm talking about. And if, like me, you've somehow managed to stay sober you know what I'm talking about. Over the last nearly eight years, I know I've had tons of people help me out of metaphorical plastic buckets, brush the sand off me and guide me towards the light. My chance for survival if I try to do anything alone is not very damn good. Hobbling along alone in the dark, whether human or sea turtle, fucking sucks. Sure, instinct will help a turtle out but we people? We need one another. 2016 felt like a never-ending process of me swimming towards the light. Despite darkness, difficulty and a brain that really wants to uses drugs and drink until it explodes, I've somehow kept swimming. From job stuff and life stuff to Orlando and the election, to the recent death of my grandmother, the battle to fend off depression and addiction and alcoholism has kept me on my muthafucking toes this year. Any more time on my toes and the damn Bolshoi will be calling me. Yet, it's all part of the gig called life; a gig I'm lucky to have. Our trip back to the nursery got delayed-twice. The not-guaranteed-but-wouldn't-it-be-cool-if sighting of a mother turtle laying eggs happened! Two gals, one successful and one who sort of fell asleep during the process and didn't really seal the deal (again, I identify), laid eggs. Just like that: more little lives, more daunting odds and more trips towards the light were set in motion. The whole journey humbled me and my own does too. It puts a lump in my throat when I think about how many people have held up the light for me. Inexplicably, dozens of folks in person, online and even people I don't know have lit the way and told me to keep swimming. If you're reading this, you are probably one of those people. Thank you for that.

Seriously. I cannot do any of this alone. I've felt so much love in the most trying and horrible times of this year, it truly knocks me out. Like those little guys on the beach in Mexico, I could do it by myself but your help makes it a fuck ton easier.

Just so you know, I'd gladly stumble around in the dark and hold up the light for you too.

No, Gracias.

"Wait, did he just offer us cocaine?" my husband asked, laughing in his beach chair.

"Probably," I said. "Welcome to Puerto Vallarta."

The sales pitch, which was lumped together with glass pipes, carved wooden bears and—of course—weed, was the first of hundreds we would receive on our eight-day beach vacation last October. While mind-blowing tacos, naps on the sand and pelicans frolicking in the surf certainly did their part in helping us forget the chaos of home, the fact remains that no matter where I go, I'm reminded that I'm an addict.

For shoppers, Mexico offers a never-ending buffet of crap—I mean delights—to buy at all times of the day. They're an enterprising people, whose kindness and convincing sales techniques have undoubtedly caused many a dazed tourist to wonder, "I don't even remember buying four oil paintings of parrots." We definitely did our part for the local economy by scooping up a cool Dia de los Muertos skull for our cat sitter, a blanket (that we didn't need, but fell in love with—because, Mexico!) and a few other must-have-in-the-moment trinkets. The variety, when it comes to drugs and alcohol, is equally as dizzying.

A couple days into our vacation, we discovered that it wasn't just that one guy selling drugs; it was sort of the entire town. The offerings were usually rattled off like this, "Pipes? Weed? Cocaine?" To which we'd politely say, "No, gracias," a phrase which becomes a musical refrain on repeat all day long in Mexico. Shrimp on a stick? No, gracias. Candy? No, gracias. Some mystery chemical that could ruin my marriage and my life? No, gracias. The reading of the daily narcotics specials was usually followed by either, "Something else?" or "Maybe later?" Sure, maybe later—like back in time before 2009, or maybe later in an alternate universe where I can drink and use drugs like a normal, non-Hemingway type.

When we ducked into a farmacia across the street from our hotel to buy bug spray, the sweet-faced girl behind the counter made sure we saw the sign proudly boasting an array of things you could buy without a prescription. And there they were, all of the stars of every celebrity overdose of the last decade: Vicodin, Xanax, Valium, OxyContin, plus cholesterol medications and an assortment of other pills that are undoubtedly cheaper south of the border. The availability and easy access to every drug under the sun isn't shocking when you consider that drugs are a huge part of the Mexican economy. It feels as normal as the men selling large stacks of sun hats. After a while, this never-ending cornucopia of drugs actually became comical. "No, gracias," we'd say but then I'd look at my husband and quip, "Maybe I'll wait to buy cocaine until after lunch?"

Travel the world as a sober person and you'll discover that the planet as a whole really likes to get loaded. In February, we were on another tropical vacation, this time on the island of St. Maarten for 10 days. Particularly on the French side of the island (where the food is better and just a tad snottier—in the best way possible), everything comes with booze. Free shots of homemade banana rum came over with or sometimes instead of the dessert menu. Wine was offered with everything and it was assumed that by renting a beach chair, you would also be drinking a dozen or so beers. Luckily, I'm married to one of those weirdos who drinks like a regular person, so I could slide any unwanted complimentary liquor his way. He also always has my back, and carefully combs over menus with me just to make sure that nothing boozy slips through the cracks. But stuff happens—as it did when we left St. Maarten to island hop to Anguilla, a tiny nation as remote as you can get. It's three miles wide with only six traffic lights, and like its neighbor, it's a drinker's paradise.

Our first night there, we had dinner in an enchanted tree-house restaurant. The joint was swanky and had the service and bill to reflect it. We scanned the menu choices in search of hidden booze and found nothing, so we ordered and didn't think twice about our choices. Every nibble during our evening was mind blowing until we got to dessert. Like any other alcoholic worth their salt, I can seriously get down on some dessert, so I salivated when I read the description of a homemade coconut bread pudding. After one bite, however, I could smell trouble. It was drenched in rum or whisky or propane or something that made me feel immediately hot and woozy. Thankfully, because of my recovery, this slip-up didn't set off a chain reaction of sketchy events beginning with liquored-up bread pudding and ending with me wandering the streets of Anguilla looking for meth. Still, I told on myself the minute I got home to other sober people who confirmed that two bites of drunken dessert weren't going to flush seven years of sobriety down the toilet.

I love to travel, but if I'm honest, I was a little afraid to do it when I first got sober. It seemed impossible. Isn't it against the law to go to Italy without drinking wine? Will they even let you inside the city of Las Vegas if you're sober? While I cannot confirm (as I haven't been to Italy and won't bother with Vegas unless I can procure free Britney tickets), I'm pretty certain that these places can be visited sober. After all, I just spent over a week in Mexico without buying drugs off the beach or slugging back margaritas. Believe it or not, our neighbor to the south has more to offer than just opportunities to get hammered—like late night baby sea turtle adventures and exploring the haunts of Elizabeth Taylor and Richard Burton who made love and fought and (probably drank like fish) in Puerto Vallarta some 50 years ago. My trip was magical, but the real reward was that I didn't have to spend my vacation trying to manage my addiction. Plus, I remember the entire vacation—which is something I can't really say about most trips pre-sobriety (including my last visit to the town where Ms. Spears currently holds court).

The world, they told me, would get bigger the longer I stayed sober. They were right. What they didn't tell me was that it would also be filled with all kinds of tempting offers, constantly challenging my sobriety. As time goes on, I discover that just like at home, all I have

to do is simply reply, "No, gracias

How to Meditate When You're Really Bad at Meditating

Sit quietly. Keep sitting. DON'T MOVE. Do this for 10 minutes. Surely, you have 10 minutes. You spend at least that much time reading your Facebook notifications. Keep breathing...Wait. Am I breathing wrong? Can you breathe wrong? Is that even possible? I need to Google that later. Hey, this feels okay. I should try 20 minutes next time. Ugh. My stomach is growling. Shut up down there, I'm trying to be spiritual. Hmm... should I have tacos for lunch? That sounds good. Maybe I just want guacamole. Is that my phone vibrating? I bet it's been 10 minutes anyway. Oh. It's only been three. Dammit.

And so it goes nearly every single time I sit down to meditate. This is particularly unfortunate, because ever since I got sober, all anyone has told me is how fantastic meditation is. There's all sorts of science that backs this up and celebrities who are big fans. So I really, really want to be amazing at meditation. My body, my spirit and most likely the other people who come in contact with me would all be thankful if I meditated more. The reality is, I sort of suck at it.

I did it once in the backroom of a coffee shop in Silver Lake with the lights turned out. It was the summer of 2010, and I was chicken-sitting (like one does in Silver Lake) and I had become a regular at a meditation meeting on Wednesday nights. It was a typical AA meeting, but with five minutes of meditation at the beginning and 20 minutes again at the end. I was trying to meditate every day for 30 minutes at the chicken house with varying success, so this meeting was a Godsend. I found it really helpful at the time, but if I'm honest, the appeal of the meeting certainly had more than a little to do with the cute, messy haired, tattooed guys in skinny jeans that could be found there. Whatever the motivation, it was helpful to meditate with other people. I mean—if all these cool kids could sit still for 20 minutes in the dark and pretend not to hear the milk foaming in the background, or the Latina girls laughing outside, then gosh darn it so could I. It's amazing what I'm capable of when I want to fit in. Plus, I was new to meditation and only 18 months sober, so hearing others share about their "practice" kind of blew my mind open.

Some people would admit that they rarely meditated, but felt good anyway. Others would share about this elaborate process wherein incense, music and the proper lighting were all employed to create a perfect meditation setting. But the ones who really ticked me off were the happy types who chirped that they prayed and meditated every day since they got sober and it's always been peachy keen with nary a day off nor an off day in sight. Well, good for them, I thought to myself while listening to their shares. I personally had to work really hard to sit still and even when I was able to tough out the entire 20 minutes (be it with hipsters at the meeting or by my lonesome), it was always a battle.

Look, I don't know if I have ADD or dyslexia or any other undiagnosed disorder from childhood that might make the simple act of sitting down really difficult. I do know that in the 1980s, kids like me always had "talks too much" or "disrupts the entire class" routinely put on their report cards. I never sat still as a child, and sure the hell didn't as an adult. As a flighty, cocaine-fueled social butterfly in my 20s and a drunk who didn't exactly want to savor the moment in my 30s, being present was never my thing. It felt overrated. Like, really. Why would I stay here and look at my life when I could be high and avoid everything?

Nevertheless, when I got sober, self-reflection is something I had to do in spades. There was so much writing, confessing and thinking about how it all went tragically awry and how I could live today differently to avoid going through it again. Prayer and meditation were just another part of this 12-step gig. In the beginning, I was totally on board. My brain was Jell-O after 20 years of drinking and drugs, so I basically did whatever people told me that might make me feel better. Praying was a piece of cake even though I'm not religious. I basically prayed to Whatever to keep me from killing myself—and it seemed to be working, so hooray for that! Meditation was foggier. There weren't ever clear guidelines or a solid how-to on the topic. (Okay, maybe there was—but I hate self-help books, and with my gnat-like attention span attending a weekend retreat or seminar on meditation was out of the question.) The only thing that ever worked for me was hearing how other people did it, even the perfect ones who seemingly never struggled like me.

Flash forward—five years later and I'm back in a meeting in Los Angeles, at one of my old haunts, with my second sponsor and a group of beloved friends. The speaker was a woman with 30 plus years of sobriety. She shared that after 29 years sober she was finally able to meditate for 10 minutes a day, 3 times a week. I exhaled. This felt like a bombshell. After three decades of sobriety, she only did this little amount? I would have thought she'd be walking on water by now and able to sit in silence for days at a time. Yet here she was, smiling proudly at her tiny, normal meditation process. Her practice sounded doable and realistic— unlike the strenuous one I was attempting back in early recovery in the chicken house. If she could be okay with just trying to meditate for a little bitty amount of time, then I could be too.

I soon started to meditate 10 minutes a day in the morning. Yes, I'd still squirm or think about what I was going to eat or watch on Amazon Prime later. The point is, like this lady (whose name I didn't even get), I was trying.

Today, I'm still sort of terrible at this spiritual practice thing. Not too long ago, my sponsor suggested, "Maybe you need to up the prayer and meditation part of your day." Busted. He has seen my brand of crazy enough times that he can spot it from across the room. He was right, of course. I've got a lot of chaos happening with juggling multiple commitments and getting ready to move, so a little extra time to breathe couldn't be a bad thing. It's the one part really missing from my recovery diet, and I've been feeling it.

The good news is, I know now that meditation doesn't have to be some marathon thing that I need to be great at every single time. As a matter of fact, I've recently discovered that it can happen in five minutes, or three or even one minute. I've even begun to get more flexible about when and where it happens. Maybe it can't go down every morning—that's okay. I can do it at work, at night or even on a walk. Also, there are some folks who say that you can't actually be "bad" at meditating. With a cellphone alarm set to a realistic goal and a little forgiveness, I'm willing to keep trying, and to me that's what being good at meditation is all about.

The Battle of Bitterville

A pot of lavender on your patio.

The guy who stands on the corner singing Motown covers.

A shaggy black dog in the elevator.

The smell of waffle cones wafting out of a downtown ice cream shop.

A text from another sober person who just wants to let you know they're thinking about you.

At the little side job I have to keep the flow of income happening, while I await that big paycheck from an anonymous billionaire who pays me to watch Netflix, there it was, the Ghost of Bitter Homosexual Future. The "cranky old queen" is a trope for a reason. This old bitch has been sipping martinis at bars and verbally assassinating anyone in her sights since time began. Wilde was maybe the first one. Capote was definitely one. Warhol? Certainly qualifies as do Crisp, Kramer and Savage (best law firm of all time, by the way). This particular real-life Bitter Betty tried to convince me how much I'll hate Portland while also encouraging me to follow him on Facebook where he "does nothing but complain about politics! It's fun!" Uh. Hard pass on that one, home skillet. But thanks for the offer!

There was an aggressive and salty quality about him the rubbed me the wrong way from moment one. Which was a bummer. There is nothing I love more than when two gay men get the "hey, sister" vibe right away and are able to kiki with each other immediately. But that was not happening here. Being contrarian for no reason other than being the biggest hater in the room is a very bitter old queen thing to do and this one was rocking it hardcore. Everything my other coworker and I laughed at, he sighed or walked away from. Even when trying to be nice to me, he seemed annoyed that I was breathing in his presence. Listen, I really wanted to give him the benefit of the doubt. I mean, I discovered he's a vegan who smokes cigarettes (lol), so I was willing to cut him some slack. But by the end of the night, I wanted to run screaming out of my little side job. Primarily, because I know that the role of bitter bitch is one I can instantly slip into myself.

The feeling you get when you talk to your mom on the phone.

Listening to your husband jam out to old school Mariah Carey in the next room.

The birds that land on your window and drive your cats insane.

So let's get this out-of-the-way: my name is Sean and I'm an alcoholic, an addict and a sometime bitter gay man. Look, I'm not proud of it, but it's like being bitter is one of our factory settings as gay men. We can all "go there" without blinking an eye. What can be charming, biting, smart and truth-telling can also easily turn into bitter and unsavory. For me, it's an ugly outfit I slip on and don't even realize I'm wearing it. After all, it's comfortable, it fits me, and it's easy to find. More than all of that, it feels like something I'm entitled to wear.

But like I said, it's fucking hideous. Still, there's a huge part of me that feels justified for being bitter. You'd be bitter too if you had my lot in life. Didn't I earn the right to be bitter after the way straight people had fucked with me since I came out of the womb in a poof of pink glitter? Maybe I'm not being bitter. Maybe I'm just discerning or critical, in the same way a one-eyed pit bull is discerning or critical. Now pass me the cigarettes and vegan meatballs along with my martini!

White Hydrangea in glass vases.

Afternoon naps while it rains.

Remembering to meditate in the morning.

Yet, as a sober person, being bitter is a big no-no. That literature that lots of sober people read says the grouch and the brainstorm are dubious luxuries for normal men but no bueno for drunks and drug addicts like me.

I've had to find a new way to live, which means I can be a little bitchy but not full force bitter old queen. For example, I gleefully like to say, "I hate everyone/everything." I don't actually mean this. I spout it off in a salty, sassy way. In an "Aww. Isn't Sean adorable? He hates everything again. Go get him a cookie," kind of way. Believe it or not, I actually see and encounter things I like and even love. Nearly every hour of the day.

The truth is, I write gratitude lists every day and have for over seven years. I find five things that made life a little better and I write them down. That's it. That is the whole practice. The end. Thank you for attending my TEDTalk. Really, it's that simple. It's a kind of magic that does not require special oils, a wand or even an ancient spell. Listen, I don't know why it makes me less of an insufferable asshole. That's why it's magic. All I know is that it does work. A little daily flow of positivity and love helps keep the bitter old queen away, maybe not entirely away but less bitter.

When I was 24, I worked at a Mexican restaurant where old gay men would sit and drink margaritas and bitch about their lives. Bobby, the bartender, smoked cigarettes and told me stories of his days on the MGM set as an assistant. He even went to Korea with Marilyn Monroe. I loved dear Bobby but she was a bitter old gal who drank a lot. I just naturally assumed this would be my destiny: Drunk, bitter and unhappy. But in the ultimate plot twist, I'm no longer drunk and I'm certainly not unhappy. I've already defied my gay programming and started to erase the writing on the wall. Hopefully, one day at a time, I can be a less bitter too. In the meantime, I'll settle for sassy and salty.

Burritos and Broken Hearts

It wasn't the end of the world. Because if it was the end of the world, there wouldn't have been burritos. See, Mexican food is at the very epicenter of my emotional core. Thus, if it should suddenly somehow not exist, I will know that we as a society are really screwed. A disturbance in the force looks a lot like a lack of tortillas and hot sauce. Therefore, I know it wasn't the end of the world yesterday because I gobbled down a burrito at lunch. It was just a broken heart.

Go ahead and mock the humble burrito, but if you're some person who thinks that random crap in a tortilla constitutes a great burrito, then keep that shit to yourself. Seriously. There's an actual art form when it comes to burritos. A great burrito is all about ratios (not too much rice, not too little salsa) and amazing condiments (homemade guac and hot sauce only). It's a delicate balance that begins and ends with a good tortilla and well-made ingredients. Don't get too fussy and in the same note, don't half ass it, either. Trust me. I'm not some pinche gringo who pretends to know everything about Mexican food. My affinity for the cuisine started at childhood and carried on through adulthood as I waited tables at not one but three Mexican restaurants. Also, being an Angeleno for 15 years meant that Mexican food became my religion and people were judged on what taco trucks they were loyal to. I had a mental map of that town based on what Mexican places were where. I even dragged my husband to the Mission district in San Francisco to try what was dubbed the country's best burrito (totally worth it, by the way). All of this is to say, when it comes to a great burrito, I know what the hell I'm talking about. Yesterday's offering, while a decent Portland college try at a Mission style burrito with its charred chicken and toasted tortilla, couldn't erase what was happening inside of me.

Getting sober sometimes means letting things go in order to get better. For me in 2009, that meant letting go of my dog Jake and cat Phoebe. I could barely feed myself and was just trying to get through the day without being loaded. It was a heart wrenching decision, but I had no other choice. Jake passed a few years ago, loved and taken care of by my ex, while Phoebe has lived for the past 8 years with my friend Regina. I got a Facebook message yesterday from her and she told me that Phoebe was being put down. At 17 years old, the girl had a good run and I am eternally grateful that she wound up being well cared for. Nevertheless, the news knocked the wind out of me. Feelings of loss and sadness bubbled up inside me. My body temperature raised and I felt like I was going to burst into tears. As usual, I'm unable to deal with any genuine emotion unless I turn it into a social media event, so I tweeted about it. Yeah, there isn't anything more 2017 tragic than tweeting and crying. "Tweetin' and Cryin'," my new country single. Still, it sort of helped and forced me to go for a walk. I went and had a cappuccino and some chocolate biscotti, but much to my dismay, they weren't prepared by a wizard and therefore couldn't make all of my sadness go away. As I sat in the cute faux Euro cafe, flipping through some shitty free newspaper, I started crying again. "Tears in My Cappuccino", the B-side. My heart was really hurting and I knew exactly why: even though I've been sober for 8 years and even though my life has changed for the better in every way possible, sometimes the past just fucking hurts. And sometimes my heart hurts too. Not just for those two poor sweet animals, either. I was also devastated for me. Poor Sean, who was so mangled by addiction and alcoholism, had to make that kind of choice. I texted my husband and cried more until I realized I better get out of this cafe before some concerned Portlander asked if I was okay.

After more walking, I wound up back at home. I didn't feel better, but at least I was tired. As if he knew how shitty I felt, Larry came and laid down on my chest. Larry, for the uninitiated, is my rascally black cat and, despite his name, not our building maintenance guy. The miracle of this moment wasn't lost on me, but the pain didn't vanish either. As I tried to turn the heartbreak off with some Netflix therapy, I finished the rest of my burrito. A few hours in the fridge did it some good and made it saucier. However, it was still only a 5.5 on the Mahoney burrito scale at best. To be fair, the kind of relief I wanted didn't exist inside of a tortilla or cappuccino cup. I sat in my bed and watched whatever the hell I was watching until my eyes got heavy. I went to bed knowing that I'd feel better today and I was right.

All of this is to say, it wasn't the end of the world. There's more burritos and more heartaches to come, but there's more miracles to come too. In the end, I'm lucky to experience all of it, even if it doesn't feel like it at the time. So for now, pass the hot sauce.

I Die a Little

IT'S A SAD-ASS state of world affairs when a chocolate mousse made with love and instruction from the divine being of Julia Child herself can't fix my broken heart. After all, whipping up such an act of selfless, culinary love on Saturday for a room full of strangers should have made me high for several days. I mean, I don't snort cocaine (anymore) so the power of a good homemade chocolate dessert should not be underestimated and under normal conditions would have done wonders. But this Saturday was not normal. Listen, you are smart people with fancy phones that tell you immediately when the world has gone to hell. Bless these little devices right now as they seem to be working like children in factories during the Industrial Revolution. You know to what I am referring. You know that for the next few days, when we talk about feeling like shit about the world, we're talking about Charlottesville. This nightmare, this hate crime, this racially motivated act of terror and as well as the stomach churning pageantry which proceeded it is already infamous. It's already another sad, shitty sidebar of American history and what we end up doing with it is anyone's guess. At the emotional intersection of Bitter Old Gay and Sober Sage, I'd venture to guess not a damn thing will change. This is an awfully negative response, but you know me; this bitch keeps it real. Anyway, this isn't that piece. This also isn't that essay about how to fix racism or the world or what people are doing or not doing. This is about me.

It's very typical of an alcoholic to turn a national disgrace and tragedy into something all about himself. Consider me guilty as charged, but in my defense, my website is entitled The seanologues, so I sort of let you know that I was my favorite topic from the jump. Look, I don't live in Charlottesville. I am not a person of color. I was not there Saturday. What I do know is, the way I process this kind of news is different than it used to be. It seems to happen in stages. For example, when I heard about it, I was at my day job. I work at one of those places where foodies come and take cooking classes while drinking wine. I'm supposed to help the chef instructors but really I just snack, eavesdrop on hilarious Portland food snobs and occasionally get to cook too. It's not a bad artist's gig, as these things go. So, when my social media blew up with news out of Virginia, my default is to snort, roll my eyes and shoot off a salty, "Well, of course this is happening" tweet. The more I read, the more annoyed I got. I had to put my phone down. After all, there was a chocolate mousse to be made, dammit.

As I plowed through Julia's extensive and exhaustive directions, the mousse materialized. There's something deeply satisfying about just following a recipe. Like, I cannot control what hell on Earth is happening right now but I can be damned sure this mousse turns out flawlessly. And that it did. After working all day and obsessively checking my phone for the latest bad news, I was exhausted. I went home, flopped on the couch, nibbled a dinner that wasn't as impressive as the mousse I made earlier and generally tried to let Saturday melt away. When I woke up on Sunday morning, it was still there. Not just the headlines and the trending topics from yesterday, but that aching pit in my stomach.

Another work shift (this time, pastas of the world!), another face plant on my bed at home where I took a nap. When I got up, "Ev'ry Time We Say Goodbye" by Cole Porter was stuck in my head. Well, still stuck in my head. I sang it softly to myself earlier in the day on my way to work. I'm lucky enough to live in a part of downtown Portland, where a gay singing Cole Porter to himself happens to be pretty basic behavior. Porter's lyrics are always a touchstone for me. When I need confirmation that beauty exists and that we are capable of truly lovely things, Cole Porter's songs always provide. That song in particular personifies Porter's masterful lyrics while revealing his tender heart. It's a song of longing for a person whose absence is utterly heartbreaking. On a day like yesterday, however, it kind of felt like a goodbye to something else. Like every time I say goodbye to our humanity, our compassion and our love for one another, I die a little. I wonder why, a little. I thought about this as I sat on the end of my bed, it happened. 24 hours later after a day of senseless and horrifying hate, I cried. And I cried a lot.

Crying is not an abnormal thing for me. In fact, I consider it a win every time I do because I lived two decades as an emotionless drunken robot. I once heard my friend Dennis, with 25 years of sobriety, say tears from sober people shouldn't just be comforted but congratulated. I wholeheartedly agree. When I respond with tears or compassion or humor, I'm working through it, instead of moving around it. In other words, don't worry about me when I'm crying. Worry about me when I tell you I'm "just fine." In this case, I feel like having emotions might be particularly powerful.

Consider this: Currently in this country, we are at the whim of blustery, unemotional, bigoted assholes. These stilted shitbag examples of white men would rather die than show real emotion or compassion for another human being. Thus, crying or going to meetings or therapy or helping others are now rebellious acts. The more we express ourselves, the more we take care of ourselves and one another, the less power they have. The first version of Ev'ry Time We Say Goodbye I listened to yesterday afternoon, before the tears rolled uncontrollably down my face, was by Ella Fitzgerald. In my sorrow, I had to smirk that the vocals of an angel like Fitzgerald (a black woman and civil rights activist), Cole Porter (a gay man) and Julia Child (an unapologetic liberal and harsh critic of McCarthyism) were the Americans I turned to this weekend for comfort. Even my artistic inspirations from beyond the grave were holding their middle fingers up while also holding my hand.

I guess the thing is this: sure, my emotions and reactions to world events are not the end all and be all. And thank God for that. But at least, I'm able to have them. So if you are upset too and have cried too, know that I get you and know that it's okay. It feels normal. It feels appropriate. After all, imagine, if none of us felt anything after Charlottesville. We'd all die more than just a little.

It's a Breeze

HOLD ON. JUST relax. It's about to get real crystal in the window, dreamcatcher, Shirley MacLaine, spirituality hippy dippy up in here. I'm going to say stuff like "The Universe" and "God" and I might even talk about magic. I promise it'll be okay and you won't want to vomit. I mean, you won't want to vomit due to what I've written but you might vomit because you ate some bad Indian food. I don't know your life. Anyway, I'm thinking a lot about these things, these topics of beings greater than myself right now and how it relates to writing and creativity.

As I was walking this morning at an ungodly hour, to go hear alcoholics yammer about their lives, I felt it: a breeze. Breezes are significant to me, believe it or not. (I know, I know. Insert eye roll.) When I first got sober in Santa Monica, there were these incredible ocean breezes. Like everything else in the greater Los Angeles area, the breezes were like "Helloooo!!! Notice how fabulous I am!" As I got to the part of the program, where I had to pick out a Higher Power, I thought the ocean was a good place to start. After all, it seemed responsible for these punch–you-in-the-face breezes and it was also enormously vast. The ocean looked a lot like God to me in that moment. Plus on that side of town, it was easy to access and find what was important to me in that particularly fucked up phase in my life. From there on out, the breezes became my higher power's way of saying, "Hey, boo. What's up? Stop being ridiculous. Love you. Byeee." My higher power and this relationship with G-to the-O-to the-D has since expanded, but breezes are still a nice way for us to keep in touch.

This morning's breeze was no different. It was a little reminder that I was fine. That everything was cool and that I didn't have to worry about running the show. The breeze and the magical force behind them had this. All of this, which was fucking fantastic news to receive via the wind, as I've been up in my own shit as of late. Now, not any more than normal for any alcoholic, but I'd be lying if I said I didn't still try to micromanage the outcome of my own life or the lives of people around me.

I've got a lot of pots on the stove right now. I don't know where all of my finances are coming from or what's going on in a few relationships or even what my career as a writer holds for me on a daily basis. It's all an ongoing mystery and as intriguing as that may sound, it's kind of frustrating for a control freak in remission like myself. Yet, this little breeze shows up and reminds me that things are already great and that I'll always be taken care of.

This is all paramount when it comes to being creative. I need all of the outside forces to work in tandem with me so I can finish projects, meet deadlines and have the momentum I may not be able to muster on my own. The nature of freelance writing is of the one-man-band variety without the snare drum or snazzy hat that my mind somehow associates with that title. Writing alone is exactly that-alone. There's no Barbara in accounting to chit-chat with over coffee breaks. There's no snarky inner-office email threads to snicker at. It's just me, the cats and the computer. Whilst I am never afraid of the well drying up and me not having anything to talk about, I do need pushes, pats on the back and gentle nudges. The cats do what they can, but they're on a tight sleep 14 hours a day schedule that cannot be interrupted by my fragile writer bullshit. Therefore, the magic of the Universe comes in handy. Any and all signs, moments of serendipity and mystical moments are requested, needed and desired. My special kind of self-obsessed crazy can't always be solved by encouraging words from mere mortals. I can't really explain what this physically looks like in real life... but it feels like the painting of a wizard on a van, mixed with the drawing of the Pegasus on your 6th grade trapper keeper, sprinkled with all this stupid and totally not reality based feeling that I am safe and protected. I know it's some weird shit. Yet it works. It works despite not even being conventional. The idea makes sense especially when you consider that I shouldn't even be here.

When I was 15 years old, I thought about leaving. Not running away but leaving this realm. Leaving is a nice way I've come up with saying I thought about killing myself. That phrase, "killing myself" sounds so dramatic. It wasn't though. I just bought some over the counter sleeping pills and I was just going to take all of them. After a blow up with my dad that turned physical, I thought it was probably a good time to leave. It was sort of that easy. Besides, I was obsessed with Marilyn at the time. She died by sleeping pills, right? She killed herself and everybody loved her. That was the extent of my plan, but according to all sorts of public service announcements and every doctor that I've seen ever, you need a plan to be taken seriously. I was 15 though. I just wanted to leave. It wasn't about impact or making a statement. Sensing I was depressed and having witnessed the violent blow up, my older brother invited me to drink and smoke weed with his friends. I shook off my tears and agreed. And there it was. Drinking and drugs saved my life. What's more, they also allowed me to leave this realm without having to actually die. It worked for a very long time until it didn't. When drugs and alcohol stopped being the force I could rely on, I had to find something, anything else.

By having faith in something bigger than myself, I can keep going. I can take risks that on my own, I would never do. I can put myself out there and know I'll be okay, no matter the outcome. This force, this mystical power, this whatever helps me feel less alone and pushes me to keep going. For creative people, that is half the battle. They say, and by "they" I mean other hippy dippy spiritual types, that you can't be in fear and in faith at the same time. To which I often reply to them, "Oh yeah? Well, I'm a multi-tasker! So we'll see about that." But they're right. I know that at the end of the day, all of it is a decision. Am I going to decide to feel isolated and solely powered by Sean's insane ideas or am I going to rely on something else?

By now, I know the answer. I know that I have a choice. It can all be miserable, even writing, if I choose to make it so, but it can also be a breeze.

PART III

PASSING & PRESENTING

Passing & Presenting

ONCE YOU'VE PISSED yourself, I'd say the illusion that you're doing just fine has pretty much been shattered. It's not really the kind of thing you can brush off and say "Oops!' Okay, maybe the first time, but once you've peed yourself a second time in less than 48 hours, everybody pretty much knows that you're not doing that fantastic. Yet that's exactly where I was a few years ago. Here I was six years sober and peeing myself while in the hospital. It was an odd place to be considering for months, I'd been telling anyone who would listen that I was fine.

Just a gnarly cold. Just pesky allergies. Just the flu. For the better part of 90 days, I desperately tried to sell a story that I was fine and that you shouldn't worry about me. Mainly, I didn't want anyone to worry about me because some sad ass alcoholic thinking still yells in my brain and tells me I'm not worth taking care of. I can muscle through whatever horrible feeling or ailment that I'm having. This all sounds like insane horseshit of the highest order, to be sure, but that's just the kind of brain I've been gifted.

Suffice to say, I wasn't fine and I was about as far from fucking okay as possible. What I had was a nearly deadly case of pneumonia, which among other things, made me too weak to make it to the restroom to go pee. Urine soaked sheets and hospital gowns as well as more than a puddle or two left on my hospital room floor were my body and bladder's way of saying, "No, bitch. We ain't okay." I text a friend, who was studying to be a nurse at the time, about how embarrassing it was to piss myself. He basically told me to shut up, that they saw stuff like that all the time and to stop texting him and focus on getting better. Pneumonia was here and it was now out in the open that I hadn't been fine in a while. The best way I can describe pneumonia is if you gave the worst flu you ever had cancer and also told it to drain your life force like an evil alien. Wheezing, having a hard time breathing, one day at work my body finally threw up the white flag and went on strike. It was like, "Lady, do what you gotta do but we're not working anymore." Carried out of work on a stretcher and rushed to the hospital, there was still part of my brain that said, "Maybe this isn't that bad." Because it's not that bad when you're leaving work early in the back of an ambulance. Nuts, but that's what was going through my mind. Once I arrived at the hospital, it was clear I wasn't going anywhere anytime soon. When everyone you come in contact with, including your own husband, has to wear some sort of hazmat mask, you pretty much get over the idea of being able to bounce out of the emergency room in a couple of hours. I was here. I was really sick. And I wasn't going anywhere.

One doctor, with the whimsical last name of Bloom, described me as "on death's door." Not entirely sure that "death's door" is the definition of gentle bedside manner, but I certainly have never forgotten it. On some level, I guess the former Goth teen in me took being on death's door as a compliment, but me the 40 something adult was mortified at. How did this person who overcame drugs and alcohol and lived with HIV, get to this point? How did this person who preached self-care and handling his business let his health fall so totally off the rails? Let me give you some background information before you say really nice things like, "Yeah, but you alone can't stop pneumonia!" or "None of this is your fault!"

As a person living with HIV and a special, high maintenance version of that disease (because why have a normal virus when you can have an Extra Virus?), I don't currently have an option of living without meds. It's a necessary evil right now, but please feel free to send me 55,000 articles about natural remedies or other ideas you, a person without my disease, might have that would magically fix me. Actually, don't. There's currently no way around me being able to function without medication. That, however, didn't stop me from trying. I had a blip in my insurance, which rendered me unable to get meds and figured, "Meh. How bad would a few months off meds be, anyway?" After all, I felt great. I had been on medication for years. What's the worst thing that could happen? A few months got closer to six months and my energy got lower and I got skinnier. Before I knew it, it was almost a year and there I was peeing on myself in a hospital room. Things were bad. Death's door, true to what you've heard about the destination, was awful.

My little body was breaking down and it would take months on an even larger combination of pills to get me back where I was. But the bigger problem in my mind with all of this was my utter inability to be real about where I was. For all this living in a program of honesty about my alcoholism, I certainly had no problem defaulting to my bullshit, "I'm FINE!" setting. A setting that damn near killed me.

Too many gay men are still dying from complications of HIV and AIDS. Too many more are dying because of alcohol and drugs. More still lose their lives to suicide and untreated mental illness. I'd go out on a limb here and say the bigger cause of death for gay men is acting like they're okay. Already saddled at birth with something that makes them different or less than, lots of us come into this world already at a deficit. We walked into this party wearing the wrong thing and spend much of our time trying to convince ourselves and others that we belong. To survive and get by, we develop an attitude of "I'm not just okay, I'm AMAZING!" and it's one that is complete nonsense. Still, it's one we need to sail through this world. We work hard to make that attitude the truth by having perfect bodies, perfect jobs, perfect dinner parties. Passing for normal, passing for straight, passing for sane, passing for undamaged, perfect goods.

For me, I was a perfect smartass. If I could pass as somebody with a whip smart sense of humor, then maybe nobody would ever know the truth. This attitude of "funnier than thou" got me out of sticky situations, helped me shrug off heartache and constructed a tough wise-cracking persona that made you laugh but also kept you at an arm's distance. God forbid you actually get to know me and know how broken, sad and horribly insecure I was. Best to keep me at the cocktail party where I could spout of zingers and funny stories. It wouldn't be wise to turn to me for anything remotely resembling emotional honesty. Part of what made hitting rock bottom so painful was the news came out of nowhere for a lot of people I loved. I had worked really damn hard to act like I was okay and that everything was FINE, DAMMIT. When that veil was pulled back, I could breathe. It was out. I was a drunken, drugged out disaster and I needed a lot of help.

Having to come out as gay, then an alcoholic, then a person living with depression and HIV has afforded me a luxury of barfing everything out on the table. In fact, much of my career as a writer is based on this very thing. A quest for the truth and the push to tell it is what drives me but obviously I fall down on that job all of the time.

The fallout for not being real about my health was considerable and not just on my body; that took years to really bounce back. My marriage was put through the test. My poor husband beat himself up for not seeing the signs. My family was once again hit with shocking news when previous reports stated that everything was hunky dory in my world. I struggled to reach out to my sobriety family who really, really wanted to take care of me because that's how they roll. Unfortunately, my act of "it's not that bad" kept them at arm's length too. As usual, I was the one suffering. I was humbled that even though I had years of sobriety under my belt, I still sucked at being honest about where I was really at and what was really going on with me. I felt embarrassed that for all my bragging about growing so much as a person, I was really still at my core, a little gay boy afraid to let you know he was hurting.

Pneumonia nearly killed me. Alcohol and drugs tried to do the same for two decades. But in the end, it's the total dishonesty and bullshit pursuit of pretending I'm okay that will 100% kill me dead. If I'm suddenly unable to say," Hey I need help. Hey, I feel like shit," then you need to be worried. I need to be worried. I need to be pis

What If I Were
No Longer Sober

What if I were no longer sober?

What if I started drinking again?

What if drugs were something that I all of a sudden just

did again?

What if this part of me for the last 8 years just melted away and suddenly wasn't?

What if it turned out to be not a big deal?

What if it could be normal?

What if *I* could be normal?

I wouldn't say I live there. I wouldn't even say I hang out there. But I would be lying my face off if I didn't say I still slowly drive by there. I'd be lying if I said I didn't occasionally look in there and see what I might be missing. I admit it. I have been known to peak in the windows and wander around a bit just to see what it might be like if I were no longer sober.

WARNING: This entire thought process, as well as the conversation we are about to have, is probably terrible for a sobriety guru and all-around spiritual inspiration to be having. So thank God I'm not one of those assholes. I mean seriously, how exhausting. I'm just some writer jerk trying to be less of a jerk and stay sober while doing so. My brand has very low standards, people, making it easier for me to pass the smartass savings onto you. If I were perfect and had totally nailed this gig of recovery, I'd pretty much have to stop talking about myself which would be a travesty. Also, I'd most likely be a robot because from what I've seen, struggles and really crazy thoughts don't stop happening just because you've stopped drinking or using drugs. Bummer, I know, but them's the breaks.

As you may have guessed, the crazy thought that popped in my mind was what if I just stopped being sober? I've been sober for over 8 years so the idea of how it would be if I suddenly started drinking again is an intriguing and terrifying one. Based on 20 years of dedicated field research, I tend to think that the experiment would be a catastrophe. Back in 2008, I had a specific period of time which illustrated this theory nicely. I had been sober for 5 months. And by "sober" I mean dry, pretty much insane and doing it myself all the while hanging out with daily drinkers. This is a god awful plan, by the way and I wouldn't recommend it. Nevertheless, she persisted and somehow managed to stop drinking. Life, however continued to be hard, shitty even. Without any real plan to stay sober, I did what I always did to deal with hard times, I drank. Things got even shittier as I added alcohol back in the mix. It was that simple. So, I know from firsthand experience what it looks like when I go back to drinking, but I have the brain of an addict and that brain is going to ask me, "what if?"

I mean, hi. Drug addicts and alcoholics think about drinking. It's what we do. So sometimes, no matter how happy we are in our sober life, we will do just that. Wondering what life would be like if I just was no longer sober seems normal. While I have no crystal ball or psychic abilities (again, bummer) I know for sure that if I wasn't sober, I'd lose connection with people. First off, I'm pretty sure that I wouldn't have the time or patience or the stomach to put up with my sober circle of friends and family. Relations with them would be counterproductive and annoying. They know too much and therefore they would have to be removed. Secondly, the re-established connections I have since I got sober would once again be wobbly due to the fact that I was no longer who I said I was trying to become when we got reconnected. Lastly, I know the actual circle around me would shrink. I needed people less the more I drank. I couldn't handle their perfect lives or judgment. Being alone is just easier.

But how long could I go on? How long before it got out of control? Would it ever get out of control? These are things I don't know and things that, for today, I don't actually want to know. I've recently watched a few friends drift further and further away from their sober selves and that's probably where this post comes from. Despite the near-click-baity title, which suggests I'm on the verge of a dramatic relapse, I'm mainly curious. What happens to the brain to bridge it from passing thoughts of drinking to slipping right back into your old life? What happens to the soul to make it shrug and think "Eh. Why the hell not?" Again, I don't know, but I do know being honest helps.

Recently, three people I love have had really open conversations with me about not feeling inspired by sobriety and not really wanting to do the work anymore. These conversations have opened the door to very real, "Oh my god. You too?!?" types of exchanges that suddenly help the task of staying sober feel less daunting and more fun. These people are alcoholics like me, whose first instinct is to tell you they are fine and that everything is wonderful. So, the fact that we're able to get real with each other and laugh about our insane thoughts is really powerful and an antidote to the very thinking that ails us. These thoughts become less scary and funnier and our bonds become tighter. Plus, and this is really worth mentioning, we're all still sober.

Conversely, I've also witnessed a few folks whose worlds have gotten smaller, whose connections are less and less. These people look like they're drifting away. They don't seem like they're doing all that well, but they also haven't opened their mouths and reached out. They seem okay going back to ideas that got them drunk the first go round with hopes that it might be different. It seems like a scary game to play, but like I said, I get it.

So, what if I'm never "normal"? What if I have thoughts of drinking or using for the rest of my life? Okay. What if I could still be happy too? What if my world could still get bigger? What if I could still feel more love than I had ever dreamed possible? And what if there's even more magic coming if I just stay sober and continue to try to get better? Now, that's a "what if" truly worth pursuing.

Approval Anonymous

I DON'T THINK I could ever be Kylie Minogue. This is, I can imagine, a relief to the actual Kylie Minogue as it means she won't be out of a job nor will she have to partake in some weird body switching thing and become a 45-year-old gay alcoholic. A little background information on where this thought comes from: On a recent sunny, Sunday afternoon, I was randomly thinking about Kylie, as one does. Mainly, I was thinking how fickle her widespread love and approval has been throughout her career, at least here in America anyway. It's like every 15-20 years we, as a country, decide that we remember that Miss Minogue is, in fact, a legend. There were no fewer than 14 years in between when she charted on these shores with a cover of The Loco-Motion and her 2002 hit, *Can't Get*

You Out of My Head. This doesn't mean Kylie wasn't out there doing her thing and making delicious pop confections. It just means our dumb American asses were too stupid to notice. I obviously have a lot of strong feelings about this major pop culture travesty. Nevertheless, this neglect from an entire nation, this utter denial of approval is precisely the thing that would knock me out of the running for becoming Kylie's replacement. The very idea of being ignored at the drop of a hat crushes me because at the end of the day, I am an approval addict, through and through.

My first drug and my worst drug, approval is something I've chased long before I ever picked up a beer bottle or crammed a straw up my nose. Who knows where it started but in my mind I think I probably made somebody laugh when I was infant, and saw how it made them happy. In turn, it made me happy and then we were off to the races. From applause garnered for impromptu lip sync performances to scratch and sniff "Grape Job!" stickers on spelling tests, I itched for validation. I ached for any sign that I was okay, that I wasn't a misfit but I was as good as everyone else. All of this sounds pretty normal for normal kids, but when you have a brain like mine, there was never enough. There was never enough love, there was never enough approval and therefore I was never enough. This is some sad, sad business for a little kid but downright pathetic for a grown up person who should have gotten over that shit.

During active addiction, a phrase I love because it makes it sound like you snort cocaine while wearing track suits and terry cloth headbands, the hunt for approval worked in tandem with the hunt for booze or drugs quite nicely. People who I wanted to be my friends also did drugs and drank, so I could relate with them on that level. I would take them hostage as friends and then ditch them when they wanted anything real from me, crazy shit like accountability or honesty. We all spoke the language of more so that meant we all wanted more. More love, more drugs, more drinks, more cigarettes, more conflict. The approval I got from them was hollow and toxic. Each of us wanted to vampire hours and days off of one another and if you couldn't meet the supply and demand, I'm sorry my dear, you were up for elimination. We also gave each other approval for behavior and attitudes that the rest of the world wouldn't put up with. Wanna have a three-way on a week night with people you met from Craigslist? We approve. Wanna verbally assassinate one of our other friends? We approve and we'll you help you out with that. Wanna drink on a Wednesday afternoon? Not only do we approve but we'll also meet you at the bar. Outside of my drinking and using friends, I scored approval where I could, by telling jokes to customers at the restaurant where I used to work, by writing little articles that people would read and pat me on the back for and by puffing up my meager accomplishments to anybody who would listen. Obviously, we all sort of exist on this planet and hope that people will love and approve of us and I hear there are normal, healthy ways of seeking that out. It's like Stonehenge. I know it exists, but until I see it for myself, it's just a thing people talk about. Without any real self-esteem, the never-ending quest for approval is fucking exhausting. Making people laugh, quick sexual encounters and-God it pains me to say this- likes and comments on social media posts all fill up that void inside of me. But without an internal approval supply, there won't actually ever be enough.

This was abundantly clear when I got sober. More than a few times, I resorted to having quick hookups to make me feel better. I wasn't looking for Mister Right. I was looking for Mister Make Me Not Feel My Life. Approval through sex is the fastest way for me to recognize that I do in fact treat this whole thing like I would any drug. The rush of having people, familiar, anonymous, in person or online, say "we like you" is one I've chased through sex clubs, bath houses, MySpace and Twitter alike. Once I got hip to the fact that I was using people and their approval just like I did substances, even though I was physically sober, the jig was up. By the way, is the jig ever down? I guess we don't talk about that because when it's down it must mean everything is cool.

Anyway, I was gifted with a buttload of self-awareness in sobriety and that sucked. All of my addict ways of looking to, ahem, fill holes, as it were, became crystal clear. This meant I knew EXACTLY what my motivation was every time I obsessively checked Twitter to see if someone liked my tweets. This also meant I TOTALLY knew what I was doing when I flirted with random people. Mainly it meant the other places in my life where I acted like an addict were exposed and sooner or later would have to be looked at. I say "looked at" and not "dealt with" because the real deal here is that I have a lot of addictive behaviors still that don't involve substances but are ones that quite frankly I don't want to give up. They're crutches to be sure, but if this need for approval and the rush get from it go away, then what?

Back in 2008, I was sober for a hot minute of five months. It was a real delight too. I was dry and not getting any help and still trying to blend in with my old drunk life. Gee, I wonder why that didn't take. I kept trying to do things for myself and talk myself into feeling better but without any real self-esteem or support, it was all sort of a lost cause. One day, I treated myself and went to a taping of the Craig Ferguson show. Since the universe has no chill when it comes to irony, it's now hilarious to me that Ferguson is a longtime openly sober person. But I wasn't headed there to hear him crack jokes about getting sober. I was there to see Kylie Minogue. In a super-rare stateside appearance, Kylie was performing a song from the criminally underrated effort, X. The track, All I See is an R&B tinged should've-been banger and one that lent itself to a great live performance. In a packed studio audience filled with gays and girls, I felt one of the few moments of joy in that excruciatingly, uncomfortable five months. I relapsed not long after seeing Kylie, not that I blame her or anything. I hated myself and didn't think I was worth getting better. No amount of imported Aussie glamour could change that.

While history will be the judge if Kylie pursuing a country tinted disco record was a good idea, I know for a fact that looking at my own addiction to approval is. With a little sober time under my belt at this point, I know that cracking open other parts of my life won't kill me and I might even make me feel better. Sure, the mere idea of seeing how I've sought out approval like I used to with drugs isn't pretty. People who know how to work on these, primarily my therapist, have pointed out that if I'm validating my damn self and taking care of me, I might not obsessively seek out approval from everyone else. It's an odd thing to wean myself off of though. Something in my mind tells me that this is one addiction I can keep. After all, nobody ever died or wound up in jail seeking out approval. Yet it's something I'm looking at and hoping to let go because that's what Kylie would do. I mean Kylie doesn't give a crap if America likes her all the time. She's a worldwide icon. She moves through this world in her diminutive, sparkle-covered body with confidence and a badass survival spirit. She doesn't need to troll for the approval of randoms. She's Kylie Muthafucking Minogue. And at the end of the day, neither do I.

Talk Normie to Me

1997 Turn Ons include: destroyed soul cleverly hidden by gregarious personality, shitfire of a childhood, mangled and/or nonexistent self-esteem, a neverending devotion to me that borders on fandom but doesn't actually look like love and a great face.

Hot and damaged. That's how I like 'em. The more baggage, the better, but nicely concealed baggage stowed in the overhead compartments of your psyche. Be removed enough or over the top enough so that mere passersby don't notice that you're rotting on the inside. Sweep me off my feet. Keep me off my feet. Keep a million miles away from anything that looks real. Screw my brains out but also pick up the tab at breakfast. Fight with me, throw punches at me, verbally tear me down but act cool around our friends. Be more destroyed than me. Take the focus off my broken heart but make sure I'm the one everyone likes more. Must have a self-destruct button that can be easily synced with my own.

When I stopped drinking, I also stopped being in love with something that was killing me. I mean someone. Really it was never about his personality, which by all accounts was lovely. Fine, explosive and totally toxic, but fuck, we were 21 and 24 when we met. We were brain damaged drunken babies. We wanted to get loaded, fuck and fuck each other up. I guess would have been okay if it was for a few months or even a couple of years, but we continued this marathon for 12 years. 12. Years. It wouldn't die even though it had no real reason to be alive. It was the *Big Bang Theory* of relationships. We tore each other down, built each other back up, couldn't live with each other but couldn't live without each other. We were both dying and the worst part about it was we didn't give a fuck. It took another eviction and an actual attempt at getting sober for me to get the courage to leave. The terrifying thing is, it could have gone on for a few more years or until one of us actually died, whatever came first.

2009 Turn Ons Include: _____

Free from him and free from me around him, I was alone by the beach in 2009. I didn't know what love was but no, Foreigner, I didn't want you to show me. That relationship kicked the crap out of me and I was gonna need a hot minute before I got back in the game. Sex with bunches of boys who didn't matter was about all I could handle, but even that wasn't exciting. I used to have sex with this totally random Persian guy who was nice enough but it was about as sexy as dropping off dry cleaning. He'd do his thing and then leave. While not the 24-hour performance of Who's Afraid of Virginia Woolf that my old relationship was, it wasn't really anything of note. In fact, I'm 99% positive that the lovely, random, Persian guy didn't write any essays about having sex with me but if he did, I hope mine was funnier. The point was, it wasn't him. It was me. I had a few very lovely and attractive guys hit on me in that time frame of early sobriety and I was too dumb, too clueless and too scared shitless of relationships or real human connection to do a damn thing about it. In an odd moment of self-preservation, I knew that I should work on myself before I invited anybody else to join this circus.

This wasn't to say that loneliness, horniness and boredom didn't cause me to seek out sex and validation from basically anywhere. Around 14 months sober, I dabbled in online dating, which sounds like something your mom's recently divorced friend Judy would say, except I'm pretty sure Judy's version didn't include blowing guys she met from Craigslist, only to wonder later if they were high on crystal meth. Most of these adventures were sex driven only and involved hours long chases to lead up to encounters that didn't last more than 30 minutes. Disappointing to say the least, but I'm an addict with a can-do spirit so it didn't stop me from keep trying. During that time, I hooked up a couple of times with one guy I met on whatever app us gays were all using before the advent of Grindr. He was in my neighborhood and he had good stories of the celebrities he'd seen working as a nurse in the psych ward. I would have hung out with him more but he got irrationally upset when I cancelled on seeing a movie with him. To be fair, the film was *Killers* with Katherine Heigl and Ashton Kutcher, so in my mind, I was doing both of us a favor. He didn't see it that way and never called me again.

Being sober and meeting gay men who weren't fall down drunks or drug addicts in Los Angeles was a problem too. I don't know who started this myth that, thanks to the magic of the internet, gay men don't drink or hang out in bars anymore, but it's some bullshit. They still drink like fish, but now thanks to the internet, they can hook with guys on their phone; some are probably on drugs too. Hooray modern convenience. Regardless, if gay men had stopped getting loaded as much as they used to, it sure felt like the same old boozy scene it had always been. After all, the guys I had in my "Maybe" file, while I was with my ex, were still drinking like they did when they were placed in said file back in the early 2000's. There was a guy in my old neighborhood of Echo Park who was older than me and an Aries and somebody I always flirted with. But after running into him at a year sober, I discovered he was a total drunk, sort of a creep and oh yeah totally in a long term relationship. Likewise, social media was still flooded with friends at beer busts or drinking at gay pride or at brunches that were really just acceptable ways to validate daytime drinking. Brunch! It's morning alcoholism but with bacon! It all felt like a tired ass world that I no longer fit in. Being smashed, grabbing a guy by the crotch and stumbling back to his place wasn't how I rolled anymore. The problem was, I didn't know how to roll any other way.

Dating dudes from the program didn't seem like an option either. Okay, it was an option. It was an option I didn't take, but honestly it was probably because it just never happened. I had bone crushingly low self-esteem, so when I sat in 12 step meetings and cried about how I hated everything, I didn't exactly think I was dancing the dance of the seven veils and luring men into my sexy web of mental illness. I was mainly just not trying to use or die. Sure, if a life fixing penis attached to a sober man presented itself during a meeting, I would have hopped on it. Yet, that wasn't the case and despite being lonely I figured it was probably for the best. I was still filtering through a lot of anger, trauma and confusion from my old relationship, not to mention the massive fog caused by decades of drinking and drugs. Love, like all the mountain of debt I ran up, would just have to wait.

2010 Turn Ons Include: Guys from normal families. Guys not in 12 step programs. Guys who don't drink before work. Guys who don't know what candy flipping is. Guys who haven't been kicked out of bars. Guys who are normal. Guys who aren't like me.

After online dating and hooking up with weirdos, I decided that all of this could wait. With only a little over a year sober, there was still a lot I was trying to get a handle on, not the least of which was my HIV. The diagnosis casually whispered in my ear, "Now nobody is ever going to love you" and I believed it. Sure, I'd be trying to puff myself up with affirmations and marathon meditation sessions, but at the end of the day, I still felt less than and still felt like love was never going to happen. I told my sponsor that I was going to chill out on dating. It was a very dramatic statement and one that I'm sure she knew was full of shit. She knew me and moreover she knew gay men. She knew that seeking approval through sex was sort of my thing and it wasn't going to instantly stop, but I did pull back. A summer of bad sex and near-sketchy situations confirmed, I had to take care of myself. I went to Colorado to help my sister with the renovation of her kitchen. Being the least handy person to ever roam the aisles of a Home Depot, I'm the last person you should call during any kind of projects like this, but my sister did it anyway and I jumped at the chance to get away from lame dating life. My job in Denver turned out to be pretty easy. Primarily, I kept her kids entertained and could be trusted with tasks like ordering the pizzas.

One night after a day of scraping the toxic cottage cheese of her ceiling, we decided to go out. A renowned booty shaker of the highest order, my sister is the one person I will always let drag me on the dance floor. Also sober and always down for whatever, she whisked me away from our construction site to a gay bar. Packed with people, the Denver nightclub was funny. See, when you stop drinking and the obsession of "Oh my god. How do I do this?" goes away, it all becomes comical. From what people wear to how they hit on one another in liquor soaked states, it's hilarious. So that's what we did, we laughed and we danced, and I flirted. There was guy on the dance floor laughing at the same people I was laughing at and getting down to the same music I was. After a long time of exchanging glances, we talked, we exchanged numbers and had a kiss goodbye. He had been drinking and that wasn't a big deal. Again, he was a gay man in a bar. I knew what I was signing up for. We made a promise to hang out while I was in town and that was that.

On our first date, he drank half a mojito. He was clearly an alien because he was doing this wrong. He should have had four of those, maybe a shot and then some cocaine later. What was wrong with him? That night, we walked all over downtown Denver talking about spirituality and travel and art and most shockingly- he told me point blank that we weren't going to have sex. Like I said, alien. It was the only explanation. Over the next several days, we saw each other a lot and when we finally did have sex, it actually meant something. After twisting my stomach in knots about revealing my HIV status to him, he in his other worldly ways was impossibly understanding about that too. Night after night of amazing dates didn't negate the fact that I had to leave town and go back to LA. I left this beautiful alien in Denver, with plans to see each other soon.

Over the next several months of phone calls and flying back and forth, what struck me was how "normal" he was and moreover how "normal" I actually was when I was with him. Honest, kind and outspoken, this vacation fling turned out to have something the newly sober me found incredibly sexy: stability. Sure, he had insecurities like the rest of us but he also didn't have my baggage and that was incredibly sexy. I think I finally saw the value to stuff I previously thought was boring. You know, stuff like decent mental health and honesty. He paid his bills and had a job he showed up to. Crazy! Plus, he was never too hungover to hang out with my family. In fact, this weirdo even seemed to enjoy them. His "normalcy" wasn't really all that normal. He was a misfit musical theater kid with lots of tattoos but he didn't have my brand of insanity. This was definitely a bonus when my old self-sabotage or insane addict brain would occasionally return and try to derail our relationship, just for fun. But I started to become an alien too. I told him when I was scared. I told him when my thoughts were toxic. I told him that I loved him, but I needed to go to a meeting so I could keep being a person he would love too. And he understood. I was his first real relationship and actually, he was mine too.

I was loving in a whole new territory: one without yelling, screaming or choking. I didn't know what the hell I was doing. I made a billion mistakes and hurt his feelings a billion more times. Remarkably, he continued to walk through it with me. It was fucking weird! But I liked it. A lot. So I tried to hang onto it because, despite what I had always told myself, I deserved it.

Relieve Me of the Bondage of Selfie

How do I look?

How do I look when I'm struggling?

How do I look when I'm happy?

How do I look when I'm grocery shopping?

How do I look when I'm dealing with family members, cleaning up cat barf, watching reality TV or cooking dinner?

More importantly, how do *you* think I look?

Luckily for me, I have the magic mirror of narcissism that is social media which answers those questions with bubbly hearts. When illuminated several times over, I have won at the game of self-worth. The numbers can even tick up in front of my eyes like flashing beacons that say, "You're doing amazing, sweetie." Conversely, when nobody gives a damn, these bubbly hearts stay clear, with no numbers beside them to alert the world that my likeability has confirmed kills. Yet recently, I reached the very bottom of the mirror and stared at the whole thing. Yes, that's correct. I really feel as though I've read all of what Twitter and Facebook has to offer. I've heard the opinions. I've had my opinions. I've seen their opinions become my opinions. I've seen them take my opinions. In fact, I've now heard and read so many opinions that none of them matter or stand out anymore, even my own. Yes, I truly think I've read it all. And what I've learned is, to quote Jon Bon Jovi, it's all the same, only the names have changed.

This is okay. I mean how many things do we all have to actually talk about? It's normal that we'd ramble on and ramble and repeat crap again and again. Besides, humans and their ability to have different spins on the same topics is one of the best things about humans. The "best things about humans" would be a great hashtag, by the way, since it appears our collective qualities are harder and harder to celebrate these days and therefore should be gathered as evidence. It would be a great hashtag if I was doing those sorts of things anymore. But I'm not. In fact, I'm not really doing any social media anymore.

Or should I say "for today" I'm not doing social media. In case you didn't know, "for today" is that give away phrase we addicts use to signal that for hopefully 24 hours we won't engage in something that is addictive and unmanageable. And by "not doing," I mean I've cut back on Twitter and deactivated my Facebook for like 2 days so far. I know, I'm practically a monk. As someone who has worked in digital content and social media for the past seven years, I guess this is the part of the post where I should talk about the virtues that social media does have. You know- the ability to bring people together from around the globe, the ability to share information quickly and the ability to make you feel bad about you had for lunch- those types of things. And they are all valid and worthwhile, but I'm not going to talk about those virtues. My problem with social media is (wait for it) me.

Sometime over the summer, after I had spent entirely too long styling a selfie for an author photo of a website that I contribute to, it hit me that maybe my relationship with all of this is too intense. Putting my self-worth in the hands of others is something I've done for decades. So much so that if the folks at MasterClass are interested, I'll gladly share my knowledge with the world for the low, low price of $90.00. We ninja level codependent people pleasers didn't need no stinking social media to wrap our self-esteem in the approval of others, but it sure the fuck makes it a lot easier! Before I had to call people or walk to their houses or show up to their events that I don't want to go to but will go to in hopes of them liking me more. Now I can just post witty, wise crap that will endear me to their hearts. In my pocket at all times, I hold the power to turn over my power to faceless others in 140 characters or less. Weeee!

I'm making light of this because that's sort of what I do when a behavior of mine has become problematic. Like, "Ha, ha, ha! Isn't it a hoot how much cocaine I can snort?" But the reality is, my relationship with social media started to feel problematic. More than once, I've ignored my husband or missed what he was saying because my face was stuck to my iPhone like a fly on the windshield. It's not a cool thing to do to my favorite person. Also troubling? Something about my dependence on it felt odd. Like here I was preaching the gospel of being sober and present in my life but all the while I had gleefully become my iPhone's bitch. Uh, what? I at the very least don't use my phone or text during meetings. I mean honestly, if I can't live without looking at it for an hour, I really need help. But nearly everywhere else I'm glued to it and that's primarily because of social media.

Even worse, I'd committed the cardinal sin of social media, the one I'd warn clients about, the one every article back in 2009 would caution against: I started to take it too personally. When the tweets of others start to feel like attacks or the vague online personalities of people you don't actually know in real life start to affect you, it's time to get a grip. After all, it's for entertainment purposes only which I fundamentally know. Yet somehow here I am. It also feels like something else. It feels hollow and immature for where I am right now. Worse for a snob like myself, my dependency on it is shamefully basic. I'm no better than our president or Taylor Swift. Look what I made me do.

So what? I grab a stack of novels and go live in the woods? It's not really an option since I have real life commitments and I hate mosquitos. Like my other addictions, I have to figure out how to treat it. Listen, my motto has always been "Why do something you enjoy, when you can turn it into an obsession?" I've been down this road with booze, drugs, cigarettes, tv, sugar, people, sex, ad nauseam. By the way, if you're struggling with drugs and alcohol and this sounds like some trivial-ass bullshit, that's because comparatively it is. Nevertheless, I know I first need to admit it's a problem, which I guess this 1200 word declaration is all about and then I have to take action. For me, action looked like deactivating my Facebook account and taking Twitter off my phone. The obsession, as the sober kids say, has not been removed just yet and I'm really starting to see how much time I was actually spending on it. Yikes. It's becoming clear how much of a crutch it is.

Suddenly, I don't aimlessly scroll like a zombie in search of little bubbly hearts. Suddenly, I don't have you to tell me how I look. Now I have to look at myself.

My Expectations
Have Expectations

Me: Also? I'm 173 pounds.

Husband: But that's what you said you thought you weighed, right?

Me: Yeah. But still. It's not great news.

The Husband: Wait. So you're upset that something you knew was going to turn out a certain way, did just that?

Me: Well, I was just really hoping to be pleasantly surprised.

Husband :(laughs and shakes head)

END SCENE

The preceding little domestic scene happened yesterday after a doctor's appointment. Without getting in to my boring ass account of my medical history, I can tell you what I wanted out of this appointment and what I got were two totally different things. My teeny tiny request that I be told that my T-Cells were off the charts amazing, I was in fantastic shape and also 20 pounds lighter was sharply denied by the Universe and medical professionals alike. Not only did I leave without the news I wanted, I left with two sore arms. My consolation to being fatter and lesser healthy than I wanted was two Hepatitis shots in each arm. My hilarious nurse informed that space was scary because, "You just don't know what's up there. For real, for real." She also told me that given my HIV status, I get extra vaccination juju meaning it would be more painful. My immediate throbbing arms backed up her theory, thus I can only assume she is correct about space too. For real, for real. But more than achy arms, I slumped out of that clinic with the kind of pain only procured by out of whack expectations.

A night at the Oscars or a full-blown apocalypse and nothing else in between, that's what my crazy little alcoholic mind wants. The humdrum results of living a normal human life are of little interest to me. Cover me in glitter or in chaos. This, as you can imagine, puts a lot of pressure on everyday living. Therefore, this doctor's appointment was doomed to fail from the start. There is no way it would ever meet what my mind had built up and I know this now, sitting calmly with my mug of coffee at my kitchen table. But yesterday, I felt defeated.

The thing is pneumonia almost killed me. Since then, I've worked hard to choke down seven pills a day and stay healthy. It's been a slog, if I'm totally honest. I want any recovery I have from anything to look like the makeover scene from Cinderella. Alas, this has been anything but. It's a slow-moving journey to feel better, which my new doctor reminded me of yesterday. My numbers dropped down really low in 2015 and building them back won't happen overnight. This also explains my ongoing energy depletion and sudden feelings of wanting to lie the fuck down. I was told that this too was going to take some more time, maybe even a year or two. Again, horrible news for an instant gratification junkie like myself. I was also reminded that my HIV has a resistance in it (which of course it does. Even my diseases are rebellious little jerks.) that makes it harder to bounce back. Not hearing thunderous applause for taking care of myself or hearing that I was 20 pounds lighter, put a cloud over the truth.

The truth is, despite lower numbers, the rest of my health is good. I'm undetectable, I'm trending upward and I'm being moved from seven pills a day to two pills. The truth is, it is happening, just not as fast as I wanted. Therein lies the real bitch about expectations and what my husband found so hilarious yesterday. I knew that I wasn't going to be 20 pounds lighter since I had recently weighed myself. I was disappointed that some unrealistic magic hadn't occurred. I'm surprised my laptop didn't just explode when I typed the insanity of these thoughts. It's akin to expecting Mariah Carey to perform at your house on Christmas Eve, even though you know for a fact that it'll just be the Holiday Classics station on Pandora. Which is to say, this is all proof positive that my expectations are rarely rooted in the real world. Why have realistic expectations when you can have mentally unstable expectations? Go big or go home and while you're at it, pretend that home is Versailles.

Later in the evening, me, my sore arms and mopey attitude got something we didn't expect: compassion. My husband, the aforementioned scoffer, hugged me and said he was sorry I had a rough day. He took me out for dinner, held my hand on our walk home and, most importantly, he helped me laugh at myself. He's good like that and he also helped me realize that things are good; my life is good. And despite fantastical expectations, my health is good. For real, for real.

Confessions of
a Dramaholic

FOR THOSE OF you keeping score at home, I have at some point in my life detoxed from the following substances: alcohol, cigarettes, cocaine, sugar (a couple of times) and drama . I slide that last nasty little drug in there because for me, it's precisely that: Conflict, chaos, pot stirring, gossip, backstabbing, general smack-talking and havoc wreaking. I love all of it and it appears to be my default setting. The highs of a super dramatic life are really high while the lows are sub-gutter level. It's readily available, with no hangover and it's one of the few addictions that can go on for decades, if you want it to. I suppose this addiction to drama is a useful character defect when it comes to playwriting, but it's an exhausting way to live a normal life.

Yes, I'm gay and yes I am from an alcoholic home. Right there we have two factors that would certainly qualify me as someone predisposed to drama. Growing up in the house I did, you never knew what was on the other side of the door, when you came home from school. I didn't wait for the other shoe to drop, it usually had already dropped, causing 70 flavors of dramatic bullshit in the process. The very nature of living in an alcoholic home requires a lot of intrigue, lying and role-playing. Nobody is who they say they are and nothing is as it appears. Again, they are great qualities for a trashy Lifetime movie, but a fall down tiresome way to live a life especially as a child.

As far as being gay and dramatic, I wouldn't say that those two things are always a given. I mean I've met some boring, level-headed, normal gay people (they exist!). But for me, it's a chicken and egg situation. Am I dramatic because I'm gay or vice versa or did I just happen to win the personality lottery? Who knows? I will say that growing up gay, I certainly had to pretend to be someone I wasn't and lie about who I was, therefore adding even more intrigue to a life that was already a Pat Conroy novel your aunt would read on vacation. No wonder I started drinking at age 14. My dramatic ass life required a cocktail (or 30) just to be dealt with.

All of this being said, and me being an individual who never really loves shouldering the blame for anything, I think *The Young and the Restless* and the television canon of Aaron Spelling are partially at fault here. I think of *The Young and the Restless* every year around this time because my sister and I were absolutely hooked on the never-ending drama happening to the fine folks of Genoa City. A soap opera like *Y&R*, as we junkies refer to it, is a wonderful thing for an addict like me. No matter what day, what month or how far into an episode, the drama was always there. It's like a bar that opens at 6am and what's on tap is your run-of-the-mill baby stealing, husband stealing, identity stealing antics. If you weren't careful you could even have your family's cosmetic company stolen like the Abbotts' did. The Abbotts are at the center of all of this dramatic foolishness on *The Young and the Restless*. Through the years, the clan had seen more than its share of drama and certainly qualify as addicts, but when we picked up the drug in 1980's, there was no one causing more drama than Jill Foster Abbott. The former hairdresser turned rich housewife is a great alcoholic character that was never an alcoholic. Jill like Erica Kane, who was doing much the same thing on another network at the time- was at the center of a lot of problems. Somehow, however, she always considered herself a victim of circumstance and in no way to blame for whatever shit show was happening to her. Sleeping with her stepson, hiring imposters to take down her nemesis and paying off the trampy girlfriends of her hot dumb son Phillip were just a few of Jill's great ideas. Jill miraculously managed to never actually take responsibility for her fuck ups and usually threw someone else under the bus in the process.

On some level, I must have thought that Jill had a great way of living because for as long as I can remember, I had created dramas that would inevitably backfire.

Lying, cheating, stealing and light forgery (it's like original forgery but with fewer calories!) were something I did from early in my teens and continued into my thirties as I drank and used. Naturally, the Jill Foster Guide to Life didn't work so well in the real world, not sponsored by Downy and not airing from 11am until 12pm on CBS. But like Jill, it never mattered who got hurt and I never really owned up to the fact that, as they say in the program, my misery was of my own making.

I'd like to say that I got sober and went through the 12 Steps and I was also cured of my addiction to drama, but that isn't the truth. More pot stirring, gossip and unfortunately a few Alexis and Krystal style confrontations have happened to me since I've gotten sober. Unlike before however the high is shorter and the hangover is god awful. I have had two really dramatic fights in sobriety that felt like the closest I've come to relapsing. In both situations, I was out of control and the drama was largely my fault. Coming down from both of those highs shook my program to the core. Please note that it took two times for me to realize that this way of living did not work. It's an old mindset that now feels utterly out of step with how I want to live right now.

I've recently seen the drama addiction from the other side. Watching others struggle with dramatic thinking or situations that they've created is really painful. I wince as I watch their schemes spectacularly backfire or witness their delusional drama based thoughts spin them out of control. I wince because I know drama is an easy thing for me to pick back up. In fact, I think it's the last acceptable drug in sobriety. If you've never been around people who no longer drink or use drugs that aren't more than occasionally embroiled in some crazy drama, then you don't know enough sober people. I think a lot of us take some time to get re-programmed. I think it takes an effort to remember that, "Oh yeah. I don't have to live like that anymore." I know for me it's a choice. One that most days, I'm really good at, but some days whether it's online or at work or with friends, I seek out drama. Which, is okay as long as I'm aware of what I'm doing so it doesn't go on happening every day at the same time, 365 days a year. I'll leave that kind of drama schedule to *Y&R*.

Use Your Delusion

THERE ONCE WAS a kid who ran a hotel managed by stuffed bears.

There once was kid who drew pictures of Snoopy for hours and hours.

There once was a kid who created intricate dramas for Strawberry Shortcake and her friends.

There once was a kid who questioned if the Muppets were just puppets like everyone said they were and wondered if they could be real.

More than that, he wondered if there was a way that everything he imagined could be real and not just for a few hours but forever. Because this kid, you know me, didn't belong here. This pink glitter crayon trying to fit in the standard 64 Crayola box, then pursued a lifetime of escape. Well, midway through my fourth decade on this planet, I figured out a way to be here, to be present and to face this thing called reality. Whoopee.

Honestly, and I have said this before and will probably say it again because I believe it to be true, I think reality is overrated. I was tough-loved in early sobriety with statements like, "You'll need to deal with reality at some point." Do I though? Really? Are we sure? Because I know lots of people wandering around LA who think it's still 1999, living the same life they've lived for decades and they've never really dealt with reality. Oh sure, they're fucking nuts and have hollow shells of lives but the point is they did it. They never faced reality. Which at times sounds pretty fantastic. I mean, have you seen reality lately? Reality in 2017 is like if that term "coyote ugly" was an entire year. You know, we took 2017 home for a night of fun and woke up next to something that resembles a hideous mythological she-beast. Each day brings a new batch of global horrors, blood curdling headlines and brain rotting stupidity. With no respite in sight, things like a gorilla dancing to a song from *Flashdance* feel like a bottle of ice-cold water in the middle of the desert. Basically, I've found myself clinging to anything that doesn't feel real but also isn't a chemical because I don't do that. Anymore.

See, as a sober person, I "get to" be present today. In case you didn't know, "Get to" is this little two-word combo me and my people say in front of pain in the ass tasks we probably don't want to do but we "get to" do because we are present and accounted for. We "get to" be sober for straight people's weddings. We "get to" show up to events we would have previously been too loaded or self-involved to care about. We "get to" be present even when we'd rather not. So here, in The

Year of Our Lord Have Mercy 2017, we all get to watch the shit show of humanity in real time. Lucky us. To misquote *Airplane!*, looks like we picked the wrong year to quit sniffing glue.

Even though I'm doing this whole reality thing now, I haven't let go of imagination or even delusion. It's actually come in handy. Sure, I'm no longer playing with dolls (yet. It's only June) but my imagination feels fired and ready to take on all kinds of creative endeavors. Meditation helps a lot with this and my practice when not entirely missing in action is spotty at best. But when I do it, my brain is relaxed and ready to make stuff. I've always had an active imagination and once I stopped using my brain as a storage locker for cocaine and tequila, it has slowly reverted back to its old self. This turns out to be amazing news for someone like me who fancies himself a writer. As long as I'm not using imagination instead of paying my bills or dealing with the real world, then I feel like it's a gift and I can spread it around.

Delusion, on the other hand, is trickier. I was delusional for a very long time in the worst way possible. When you think drinking seven nights a week and not paying your bills is normal, delusion is kind of an issue. So much of an issue in that when I first saw the word mentioned in the Big Book, I bristled. It felt like a very personal dig and something I didn't want to admit that I was. But the longer I stayed sober and the more I became aware of my delusion, the funnier it got and I realized that delusion is not without its merits. I think in order to succeed on some level, we have to a have a tablespoon of delusion. We need a tiny bump of the stuff to convince ourselves that we're talented enough for a job that maybe we don't have the on paper qualifications for. A sprinkle of delusion helps too, when choosing to see the sunnier side of situations and people who could otherwise be perceived as hellish. Delusion could even be something that helps erase parts of our past.

Take, for example, dear Axl Rose. Lovingly referenced in the title of this here essay, Mr. Rose had a long and storied slip into big time delusion about nearly everything. His career, his music, his popularity, his face. Yet like a rock phoenix in jeans two sizes too small, Axl is back on tour with Guns N' Roses and even sings with AC/DC occasionally. Though big career belly flops, legendary wack-job behavior and the music industry going in the toilet had left Axl and his music in the dust, his personal delusion that he was still the rock god of yesteryear put him back in the spotlight. Sure, nostalgia has a lot to do with that but Axl being one of those deluded people I mentioned who thinks 1999 never end doesn't hurt either.

As both a writer and a sober person, I can have it both ways. I get to show up and I get to be honest about being an addict and alcoholic. Also? I'm not delusional about my past and now think it's all sort of amazing in a harrowing, awful but fabulously funny sort of way. In a second act twist I couldn't have ever written, I'm now even more creative and imaginative than I ever was on drugs or while drinking. Despite being lost, I found my way back to telling stories and being creative. I'm sure the little kid who ran the hotel managed by stuffed bears is thrilled that I did.

Forbidden Happy

You're okay. You're okay. You're okay. You're okay.

You're okay. YOU'RE OKAY.

I had to keep saying this to myself as I laid in bed. I had to keep saying it before I even had a chance to let another thought into my mind. I had to keep saying it not just because I knew it was true but also because saying it was helping. See, I woke up sweating, with my heart racing, and generally having that feeling I was far from fucking okay. As I closed my eyes (You're okay. You're okay. You're okay), I tried to believe it. I mean really feel like I was okay. My heart eventually took it down a few notches. I started to breathe normally. And right on cue, one of my cats laid on my chest. We were okay. I am actually okay. That was the truth. After all, this isn't some old feeling I had years ago, although waking up in terror thanks to years of delightful things like depression, addiction and PTSD is an old familiar feeling. No, this happened this morning.

It happened this morning at what could arguably be considered the height of my personal okayness. Fuck okay. My life has currently transcended to fabulous. New job, great relationships, strong connection to my recovery and the incredible people in it, plenty of food, money, coffee and all of those things I need to survive.

So why did I wake up there? Why did feel like I used to when I would wake up to the shitstorm of my life during yet another body crushing hangover? Why, after nearly nine years, did I wake up convinced for even a few moments that I wasn't okay?

The easy answer? Blame it on the wiring. Much like blaming it on Rio or blaming it on the rain, blaming it on the wiring for people like me with mental health, uh shall we say, "challenges", is the easiest route. Just because I am better and continue to grow doesn't mean I'm going to have the thoughts of a totally sane and healthy person all of the time. The default setting of HOLYFUCKINGSHITEVERYTHINGISTERRIBLE is a tough one to override. For my first three or so years sober, I woke up like this every Saturday morning. Except it was worse. Spritz the feeling from the other morning with about a gallon of terror and dread and you get the picture. Years and years of waking up hungover and barely human on Saturday mornings left me raw and afraid to get out of bed in early recovery. That feeling in my chest that my life was the worst and I was a piece of garbage was a nearly impossible one to shake off. It's only recently that Saturday mornings have felt normal, happy even.

Is all of this anxiety and self-loathing better than it was in 2009 or even 2015? Hell yes. Does it still exist? Do I still struggle with a brain hell-bent on self-destruction and misery? Also, hell yes. The thing is, there's a bunch of healthy stuff I do to drown that voice and those feelings out and I can currently say that all of those things are working. Perhaps it's a glitch in the system and one that won't last. I mean, I already feel better sitting at my kitchen table writing and drinking coffee. Yet it could also be something else. Something more ingrained. Yesterday, I was walking home after hanging out with someone from my recovery family. Fall leaves crunched under my feet for the first time. The air was warm but crisp. The quickly vanishing sun had turned downtown Portland a peachy orange color. The world in that moment felt beautiful. Life felt beautiful. Moreover, I felt really, genuinely, no bullshit happy. Happy with no exceptions. Not the kind of happy that's temporary or faked or delusional. But legit happiness. Short of bursting into a musical number, I walked home happier than I can remember being in quite some time. These are moments worth cherishing and remembering. Not because there was some big material payoff or splashy life milestone. But because a person like me can feel this way and can feel this way most of the time. It's also worth remembering because there's still a teeny, tiny part of me that thinks I don't deserve this: That I shouldn't be happy and that I should go ahead and do something to fuck it and up and sabotage it because it's not like it's going to last anyway, right?

My idea of happiness, much like candy-colored, ridiculous Lisa Frank pictures of unicorns, is decidedly twisted and out of whack. A dedicated addict, I want happiness to be bigger and last longer. I want happiness to be like one of those 11 minute Donna Summer remixes. I want happiness to be like crystal meth but without the paranoia and face picking. I want happiness to never end or if it does it ends with a giant musical number. I remember being 20, roller skating at a rave high on ecstasy and thinking, "This! I want to feel this all of the time!" Besides being expensive, incredibly tough on my brain and spinal cord and completely unrealistic, this version of happiness was artificial and not meant for daily living. God. Can you imagine being high on ecstasy all the time? Actually, I can, and that's my problem. Right away, I've set myself up for something that can't happen or at the very least is not in any way sustainable. Thus, when I don't live a life that feels like an endless loop of someone winning both showcases on The Price is Right, then I can go ahead and choose to feel fucked up, sad, and miserable. Waking up with a pit in my stomach might just be something that happens to me for a while. Maybe even the rest of my life, which is fine. I no longer wake up with body crushing hangovers, so what's a little occasional morning dread now and then? I destroyed my brain with drugs and alcohol through Reagan, Clinton and two Bushes. There's bound to be some reverb.

The thing is, now I know the truth. Even when my heart pounds and I'm filled with despair and panic, I know the truth. Even when I feel like I'm the worst person to walk the face of this earth and I shouldn't bother getting out of bed, even then I know the truth. The truth is that I still live in a body and with a mind who are still trying to shake off their past. The truth is, I'm allowed to feel panicked or depressed or even filled with dread. This shit passes if I let it. But mainly the truth is, despite what my brain tells me, I'm okay, I'm okay, I'm okay.

Seasonal Alcoholism

The people on the patios. Oh, the people on the patios.

All the oh, so many people on oh, so many patios. They

drink on the patios. They smoke on the patios. They

drink even more on patios. In fact, they drink so much on these quaint little patios that you start to wonder if anybody anywhere does anything else on patios. Oh sure, you might see a half-eaten order of some pedestrian artichoke dip on the table or a few barely picked at hot wings. But these people are really on these patios to drink. They so look comfortable on these patios too. Like the minute it gets warm, the people defrost, as if they've been sitting there all winter. Like they live there. Me? I just walk by all these patios. Sure, I can sit with the sober girls and drink our iced coffees but we quickly move on. We're not meant to linger there. It's no longer our turf and we know it. The patios already have their people and we are not them. And sometimes, God help me, I'm like fuck those people on those patios.

A newly sober friend and I were talking at the tail end of winter about what a trap the allure of patio drinking is once the weather warms up. We mainly laughed about how a quick trip to have a few drinks on a poor unsuspecting patio turned into a real life drunker version of Sondheim's "Ladies Who Lunch." Perhaps not just drunker but gayer. Like "Ladies who Lunch" at a leather bar. Shots, cheap beers and a restroom handjob–and one for Mahler! Something about patio drinking just seems like it's something we're supposed to do though. I mean every episode of *House Hunters* has at least one scene of a lady with bad hair saying, "I could just picture drinking wine out here, couldn't you, Chad?" As if entire pieces of property were sold strictly on how cocktail friendly their patios were. Maybe they were and it actually doesn't sound that insane. I've bought a lot crazy shit to further facilitate my drinking so buying a house with the perfect outdoor space to get loaded in isn't too much of a stretch. The pull of patio drinking is just that strong, y'all.

One day at like 6 years sober, I called my sponsor in Denver and blurted out, "I walked by a patio and people were drinking margaritas and it looked like a really good idea!" I was freaked out that momentarily my brain was so easily romanced back into the pull of patio drinking. He laughed and reminded me it was summer and I was an alcoholic. But it isn't just the patios of summer that are a trap. It's also the weather. When I lived in Los Angeles in a series of apartments with no air conditioning, something I would not recommended, I convinced myself for several summers that I drank more during that season so I could pass out at night. Surely, I could have gotten a swamp cooler without the amount of tequila I drank but who had time for logic when it was SO HOT! Summer also brought about outdoor festival season in Los Angeles which was really just a great excuse to drink outside. The same goes for backyard barbecues, Fourth of July and outdoor sporting events which I of course do not attend but don't get it twisted I definitely found myself at more than one Dodgers game based solely on the allure of beer and hot dogs alone. Summer and drinking just went hand in hand yet for a dedicated drunk like myself self, couldn't that be said of all seasons?

I remember an episode of Oprah (how every great story in literature starts, by the way) with Kirstie Alley.

The *Cheers* actress and Scientology devotee is something of a mental health barometer. Ask yourself is this something Kirstie Alley would do say or think? If you answered yes, please pause and rethink whatever it is your about to do. However, in this particular interview the star of *Look Who's Talking* and *Look Who's Talking Too* said something I'll never forget. She was spending an entire hour with La Winfrey discussing her weight which is such an odd thing that we ask actresses to do. This entire genre of interviews and books that are basically "Former Hot Star Became A Pig But Then Became Hot Again!" is just fucking bizarre to me. But I digress.

Anyway, she had become hot again and she was telling Oprah that for her, binge eating really started around Halloween with the trick or treat candy her kids brought home then it went right into all the delicious food for Thanksgiving which lead to candy and cookies at Christmas which lead to a big dinner on New Year's which lead to Valentine's chocolates which lead to, well you get the picture. What the beloved star of *Veronica's Closet* was trying to illustrate was her pigging out really didn't get a break and the mere idea that Halloween was a trigger was laughable. My drinking, much like Kirstie's eating, was all-season and her story was immediately identifiable. Stars–they're just like us! I didn't actually need it to be summer or Halloween or Easter to get drunk. Sure, those things made it easier for me to hide behind the guise of being "festive." But I was just as happy to drink alone on a bland Wednesday in August and that was the truth. The allure of summertime drinking wears off quickly when I remember it usually lead to summertime vomiting or summertime screaming matches in parking lots. Oddly enough those things usually came along with springtime drinking and holiday drinking too. Getting to that place, snaps me back to the reality that it isn't the patios who are the problem. It's me.

I guess with now nearly a decade sober, I should have some bravado about reclaiming patios. I should start a movement so formerly drunk people can now sit on patios for as long as they want, dammit! But that sounds like a lot of work and sort of dumb. Like maybe people sit on a patios for so long because they're hammered and can't stand up? Or maybe it's too damn hot to sit outside for my delicate ass anyway? But maybe me and my sober girls have our iced coffees and bounce off of summer patios because we have shit to

do, honey.

The person feeling
it the most

WHEN YOU ARE the age of homosexual that I am, you

might find yourself at dignified little chamber music

concerts. These casual yet civilized affairs will also find

you amongst people who are around the median age of

62. This isn't ageism or old people shade. These are just

facts, ma'am. Let the record show that I enjoy being

around older people. I feel free to doze off in public, fart loudly at my leisure and wonder aloud if a long line is a conspiracy against me. Oh and don't think it hasn't dawned on me that by hanging out at gatherings filled with old people, I'll always be one of the youngest people in the room. I figure, I have a decade or so on the symphony circuit until I have to upgrade to parties at senior centers and eventually just chilling at cemeteries. This isn't lost on the old people attending said events, by the way. Recently, I found myself at one of these concerts and an excited photographer ran up to me as I awaited my husband to return with burgers and brownies. "I took your picture as you walked across the lawn. Is it okay if we use it in our membership catalogue next season?" she asked breathlessly. I nodded sure because I'll take any low to no paying modeling gig as long as it means I'm forced into people's mailboxes against their will. "Oh fantastic! We desperately need photos of cool young people," replied this photographer lady who I was now going to be forced to marry. She bounced off in search of other young souls to capture on film and I continued to wait for my burgers and the person I was actually married to.

As I perused the lawn in front of the concert hall, I noticed it was filled with two types of people (old people). There were the ones who were there for a social thing and it's because it's what people their age did. This is the majority at things like this. They travel in packs and meet other packs there. They go every season and know everybody else who goes every season. They volunteer to be helpful and useful and stuff but mainly to see what's going on with Judy's new knee or Barbara's upcoming trip to Jerusalem. The other group is just here for the music, dawg. They didn't come to chitchat next to the complimentary dish of cough drops. They came to get their Bach on. They talk about each piece. They gasp in disgust when they see someone texting.. They don't need a program to kill time. They need a program to study and discuss.

It's a classical music no-no of the highest order when you applaud before the piece is over. Sure, they might take a long ass break in between songs but your ass should not, under any circumstances, get up and hoot and holler before the darn thing is officially done. But this lady the other night, the same night we became photographed for our youth and beauty, couldn't help herself. She had that hair that old ladies have. It's not like a high and tight Shari Lewis white woman afro nor is it the old rollers and curlers *Mama's Family* coiffeur. It's more like if Streisand's character from a *Star is Born* feel asleep for 40 years and woke with a softer, looser curled look of her 70's do. Wearing something pink and maybe printed and perhaps a few glasses of Riesling in, this gal was the human version of a record scratch when she loudly clapped when she wasn't supposed to. Eyes darted in her direction. People silently shook their heads. Even my husband, who knows a thing about this classical music world, rolled his eyes at me like, "Can you believe the nerve!" I nodded in agreement, but truth be told, I don't blame the bitch. It's really hard to know when that shit is really over. Anyway, the musicians didn't notice and they kept playing. I however noticed something else about this chamber music superfan. As the music went on, she swayed to every piece. She moved her head dramatically back and forth when the strings picked up with serious force. She closed her eyes in quiet moments and exhaled loudly. This woman was FEELING IT. She was feeling it so hard that I felt bad for not being on the same page. It wasn't that she was being ignorant when she erupted in applause at the wrong time: she simply could not contain herself. When everybody else is on a mild sauce packet and somebody like her shows up all three packets of Fire sauce, it stands out. It's something you notice. It looks weird and out of place to watch somebody's enthusiasm boil over when everybody else can barely summon a simmer. It's uncomfortable and awkward and maybe even inappropriate and it's definitely an attitude I want in every pocket of my life.

Okay, I know. Way to be a total addict and to want to feel over the top excitement all the time, but I'm not sure "feeling it" is even about that. Feeling it doesn't mean loving it. Feeling it to me means being present, 100%. Now whether or not, lady with loose Garfunkel perm was feeling it with the aid of chemicals, is none of my business. But to be present for things and in the moment for things, like she was, is something exotic and aspirational to me. When I think of the dozens of concerts, plays, vacations and parties I was unable to feel anything for, it bums me the hell out. Depression mixed with alcoholism and addiction meant I got excited about upcoming things and wanted to feel every moment but usually wound up too wasted to feel or even remember anything. I wanted to be the person who was moved to tears at a performance or who shouted BRAVO! so loudly a room froze, but I could not. I also, on a sadder more regular level couldn't be present for simple things conversations with friends or quiet moments alone. My brain was a scrambled inebriated mess. The only thing I was feeling was low-grade daily terror rotated with bone crushing despair. When I was moved by something or someone, I quickly poured liquor or drugs on the moment and it instantly became less than. The authentic moments of feeling it were dulled, muted and even gone. It was impossible to be the person feeling it the most when you worked hard at not feeling anything at all.

As a kid, I cried at movies, got goosebumps when I listened to records, and clapped when I watched anybody perform anything on stage. That kid has slowly started to come back. I remember watching *Arrival* a few years ago on my birthday and I jumped at the twist midway through. I was on the edge of my seat for the sci-fi parts and the emotional center of the film left me in tears. I felt all corners of that movie and Amy Adams was my guide. That year, I cried at *Moonlight* and *La La Land* too, proving I could now feel it the most on several occasions and in several different places.

A few days ago, we were once again outside at another random summer event. This time it was fireworks in upstate New York. There was a young girl working the Jamaican food booth. Without a question, she was certainly, hands down the person at that event who was feeling it the most. Despite being 4,000 degrees outside and the music in the background was a band, who was playing "your favs from the 80's, 90's and today!" according to the poster, she did not stop smiling and dancing. A Bruno Mars cover? She had the moves. A Guns 'n Roses cover? She's on it. "Cake by the Ocean"? No problem! So happy and shaking it so hard while at work, mind you, she made us forget how hot it was and briefly consider Jamaican food before we ran into an ice cream cart. Marketing strategy or actual life approach, it kind of didn't matter. This girl was another reminder that I have a choice. I can grumble about the heat or the bad cover band. Or I can shut up and shake my ass.

PART IV

DO IT AGAIN

Enough of Never Enough

WHEN DID IT start? How did it happen? Was it childhood? Doesn't it always come back to childhood? Surely, that was it. Although, maybe not. After all, I never went to bed hungry. I always got everything on my birthday list. The lights were never out and the house was always warm. By those standards, I always was taken care of and had enough. A deeper no-nonsense part of my brain, that maybe I don't want to listen to right now on my first cup of coffee says, "But did you have enough love?" Damn, girl. I don't know. Probably not. But whatever it is, I have a brain that tells me I don't have enough.

Scarcity feels like a shameful and dramatic word for an American like me to use. Here we are in the land of endless crap with more people than ever. How could we possibly feel scarcity? Google News search "scarcity" and you'll come up with some places that deserve that word. Places in India with water scarcity or places like Libya with food scarcity. That's some real shit. My buried deep inside of me scarcity, and I know this already, comes solely from me. My scarcity exists because I let it. If I am not hysterical and if I am willing to see the truth, I know for a fact that I have a house, food to eat, regular income, medical care, etc. Still, as an addict, who lived so long waiting for the next high, re-wiring my brain out of scarcity mode is fucking hard.

I promised myself years ago, when I started writing about life in sobriety, I would talk about everything. Thus here we are talking about finances, careers, jobs and other sorts of things that make me feel icky. Which is funny because I have no problem blurting out 700 words about doing meth or feeling insane, but talking about this stuff feels particularly vulnerable. I don't know why. I guess because I have this notion that a person my age should have their shit together financially. My ego wants you to think I'm some baller or at the very least a person who doesn't have single digits in their bank account. Yet the real truth is I've always been pretty terrible in the financial department. Naturally, as an addict, I have the myriad of overdrawn accounts, evictions and bad checks in my past. But now 8.5 years sober, I still struggle to balance my finances and make enough money.

Since moving, my employment status has been all over the place. Piecing together freelance writing gigs and side job shenanigans has been harder than I thought it would be. Sure, some of it, as my husband reminds me, is the new city deal. His job brought him here, however I moved here without a job. Therefore, he assures me, it's normal that I'd have a period of readjusting. And he's right. Plus, it isn't like I've had zero opportunities and no money coming in. Just not enough to really cover my bills. I've been proactive in the meantime, however. I've applied for tons of other jobs, submitted writing to all kinds of places and I've signed up for every depressing and bleak job website and their respective (and equally terrible) email newsletters. In general, I've run around like a crazy person to make it click, to make this click, to make me click into a place where I feel like I'm contributing and where I don't have to worry. And the result? Nada.

So many "no", "no thank you" and plain old no response answers have beaten me into a place of submission. I've even readjusted the goals, widened the net and tried different things. The answer has universally still been the same. Sigh like for two hours sigh. Yesterday, I had a moment. It was a hard moment but a good moment. In this little moment of mine, it hit me. It wasn't that there isn't enough jobs or enough money or that the city of Portland is conspiring against me from financially succeeding. It was me. It was this broken brain hell-bent on scarcity that was causing the issues.

Damn, girl: the sequel. "Things" were not going to change unless I changed my thinking.

Oh goody. Another opportunity to look at patterns of thinking that no longer work. I can't wait! Yet it feels like the only way. The external is not budging and doing what I want it to do, the hateful bastard. It's up to me. To be completely honest, I am not even sure what this will look like. More meditation, more faith, more gratitude all seem like the place to start. Changing my bitch ass attitude about the jobs I do have and about the money I do have coming in is another thing I can do too. But the rest of? I really don't know. What I know is this: I'm hitting a bottom around this lie of scarcity and this fraud that I don't have enough or that I am not enough. From what I know about hitting bottom, it's an excellent place to start and the only way

from here is up.

Action! I Wanna Live

WE ARE IN the era of the topless, body-positive Instagram post. We are in the era of the multi-tweet thread chronicling everything from an individual's heroic battle with a mental illness to a harrowing account of waiting in line at the airport. We are in the era of blogs routinely using (or abusing) their pages to become a digital dumping ground for confessions, neuroses and run-of-the-mill epiphanies. As a big fan of all of these things, I will say respectively and from the most spiritual place possible, fuck this era. Fuck this false sense of heroism for simply being a human who handles their emotional shit. Fuck this bar for being so low that we now spring to our feet anytime someone is real about themselves. Because for people with mental illness, addiction and alcoholism, this brand of self-truth telling isn't some breakthrough, handpicked specially for a Lenny Letter essay. It's just how we stay alive.

Hopefully, my flagrant flinging of the f-bomb didn't frighten you off. I swear all of this is on my mind for a reason (cue the aforementioned confessional in 5, 4, 3, 2...). While I like to think it takes guts for me to yell into the void of the internet, "Ugh. I feel shitty and I kind of hate myself/everything else!" I know it's ultimately chicken shit. After all, I could whine for days digitally (and I have and thank you for reading, by the way!) but if it's not happening in real life and if I'm not reaching out in the real world, it's all for show. While bleeding on the page and essentially throwing glitter on my hot mess mental health is sort of my thing, it can't just be a blog or a series of tweets. I mean for me. "For me," in case you didn't know, is what we say so we don't alienate people who are doing something else to treat their own hot mess mental health. But in this case, I don't know if it is just "for me". Study after study, book after book has shown that people with the stuff I have, tend to feel better when they share it with others who have the same thing. All of this is to say, that yesterday, live and in person without editing or a delete tweet option, I let it out.

The "it" in question is some boring, old financial and career blahs which has morphed into generally feeling horrible/depressed/over everything. All of this has been plaguing me for several days. Plaguing is a dramatic word and not at all accurate when considering places like Syria or Venezuela or Chechnya. But I described it to my husband as a "baseline of annoyance and depression". In other words, I've been a fucking delight. Completely wrapped up in self and miserable, I forced myself to go to a meeting yesterday. It was a gay meeting not unlike the gay meetings I got sober in Los Angeles back in 2009. Gay meetings are awesome, by the way. Not only do I find them to be a little more entertaining and honest but they are filled with people who get me in a way sober straight people do not. Anyway, after hearing lots of stuff that resonated, I vomited out everything that I was feeling. While the details of this monologue are best left in the magical ethos of the sacred spaces of 12 Step rooms, I will say that I felt better almost immediately. More than that, a few people gathered around me and gave me their phone numbers after the meeting. After a tear filled text session with my sober bestie in LA, who hilariously called me controlling and called alcoholism a cunt, I started to feel human. I calmed down. I ate bread and watched reality shows. I snuggled with my husband, who currently deserves some sort of trophy. I went to bed. But I went to bed knowing that I need to be in a new state of action.

The thing is, I've been going to meetings and doing the work I need to do to stay sober since I moved to Portland, but clearly I still need more help. This is always a drag for me discover. I really, really hoped that when I got sober, I'd only have to ask for help once and only feel shitty for a small period of time and the rest of my life would be like the last 3 minutes of *Gentlemen Prefer Blondes*. What I've gotten in reality is a life that actually looks more like the last 30 minutes of *Postcards from the Edge* which is to say not perfect, challenging, and a lot of work if I want to stay healthy and happy. Yesterday's breakdown/breakthrough was a wake-up call to do more work and to keep going. Therefore, I've committed to 30 meetings over the next 30 days. I'm also going to find a sponsor and take on a service commitment. I traditionally don't like to do any work and will only do so when I'm in a considerable amount of pain so consider this me screaming, "Uncle!" I guess the point of this yet-another-act of internet heroism is this. my mind was in a dark place. A sad place. A despair filled place. A fucked up place. And was kind of there for a while and was pushing me to feel like, "Why bother?" This freaked me out. Because how long do I think like this until I then start thinking that drinking or using or god forbid suicide all sound like awesome ideas? Yikes. So I told the truth. I told on myself. I cried in a basement of a random Portland church. I asked for help. Again. I did it, not because I wanted applause but because I want to be happy and alive. And because it's what we do.

Checking Out

IT REALLY ANNOYS me when people say, this, that or the other is as addictive as cocaine. I don't know what kind of bunkass cocaine y'all have been doing, but quitting sugar or Facebook or jerking off is not nor will it ever be as addictive as cocaine. Let's stop trying to make that happen, m'kay? For people with my pedigree, this sort of off the cuff shit is offensive. Like really Amanda from Glendale? I don't think you've licked cocaine off a stranger's cock or needed it just to get through a shift waiting tables, so don't tell me how hard your Instagram detox is. Or maybe you have and never developed the dependency I did. How dare you. Regardless, let's knock it off.

While we're at it let's stop saying _____ is the new smoking. Netflix is the new smoking. Meat is the new smoking. No. No, they are not. There is only one evil ass damn near impossible thing to quit and that's smoking. Just like we wouldn't say so and so is the new Darth Vader. No, bitch. There's only one Darth Vader and he's an evil bastard. Smoking is the same. One of my old coworkers read that sitting is the new smoking so she started standing at her desk. Good for her never had a cigarette in her life ass. But I have quit smoking, so I sure the fuck continued sitting down knowing there's a distinct difference between these things. After all, I never had to scrounge for quarters just so I could sit my ass down. Yeah quitting things is hard, normal people. Welcome to our entire life. Like I said, it really annoys me.

The thing about quitting things is that once you quit lots of stuff, it gets harder and harder to check out. You know, like check out of this planet? Check out of life? Check the fuck out. People worried about sitting have no idea what checking out means and that's okay. I envy them. Not about the sitting thing. My dainty behind will sit and enjoy it, just to spite them! I'm talking about never needing chemicals, drugs, sex, things to make roaming around this planet a little bit more tolerable. What's that even like? I can't imagine looking at a chemical or person or activity and not think, "I enjoy this now, but how long until it becomes problematic?" Checking out is my favorite thing ever. Not feeling life. Missing entire chunks of time due to overindulging? Heaven. There's an episode of Dukes of Hazzard where Daisy gets amnesia, and I remember thinking that sounds awesome. Not knowing who you are, being blissfully unaware of the world around you. Perfect. At least I think it was Daisy. Maybe it was Bo. I was like 8. Also? I did a lot of drugs and erased most of my mind, so see? I was successful at my mission of checking out. Hooray me. Too bad the brain fallout of such a kamikaze mission is that now I don't remember what time I'm supposed to be places or where my phone is. Pray for my husband.

Now that I don't smoke weed, don't snort cocaine, don't do hallucinogens, don't drink, don't smoke cigarettes to paraphrase Adam Ant, what do I do? I mean did I just get sober and instantly embrace the idea of being ultra-present for all of reality all of the time? Christ no. That sounds hideous. Sure, sobriety has given me the gift of being okay with life as it unfolds and blah blah blah, but at my core I'm a person who doesn't like to feel his life. Now, I'm still that person without chemicals and a buttload of self-awareness. Delightful! Therefore my first true loves in sobriety were sugar and caffeine. I'm very entitled and protective about my relationship with these two. Coffee swilling, brownie munching, loudmouth is kind of my aesthetic and I'm not looking to change. After complaining about my lack of sleep, my therapist not long ago suggested cutting down on coffee. He's remarkably still my therapist but it's still touch and go. I love coffee and I live in a city that loves coffee and I hang out with other addicts who love coffee. It's my thing. I currently have a bag of coffee in my backpack as if it were a lavender sashay that I'm planning on giving my sober cat sitter. Maybe. I have cut down on coffee or gone through periods of awareness of how out of control my relationship is with it. I quickly snap out of that silliness though and go back to pounding coffee like some 1940's bus driver. I've drunk so much cold brew I felt like I'm having a stroke. I've had so much coffee that it starts to work in reverse and make me tired. I've had to go get coffee for the next day even when it's late. I worry about not having enough coffee to get me through a day. No, that doesn't sound like an addict at all. I know this and I'm okay with it. Maybe I'll hit a coffee bottom, a phrase that sounds gross and oddly like a sexual fetish and one I promise never to use again. Or maybe I won't ever hit bottom with it. For the time being, I'm in denial that it's even an issue so we know that can last a while (forever).

Sugar, on the other hand, is one that comes and goes. I have quit sugar with no issues. Okay, not no issues. Maybe more than a few issues. The most recent time, I quit, a lethargic week or so signaled that my body was hooked on the stuff while my dreams filled with Reese's peanut butter cups, proved my brain wasn't much better off either. As a baker and a foodie, I'd like to think my relationship with sugar is just enthusiastic, celebratory even. I used to like to think that way about my relationship with wine too. I remember my first Easter sober, my brother's family all went to sunrise mass. Me and my three year old niece stayed home and ate Easter candy like alcoholics. By 8am, we were spun out like Utah tweakers at Wal-Mart, but by noon we were both whiny and ready to lie down. The out-of-control-ness of my relationship with sugar can be judged by the amount of foil chocolate wrappers found in my pockets. Like caffeine, I've eaten so much sugar in sobriety I wanted to barf or cry or pass out. I've started eating cookies or Halloween candy and not been able to stop. Like I said, the kid's still got it.

The societal okay of binge watching came about just as I was a couple years sober. This was fabulous for me, the former movie nerd who'd watch six episodes of the

Brady Bunch to avoid people or doing homework. Now everyone was doing it and it was fun! Wee! We're all hooked on something together! Yay! Binge watching for me is like snorting Adderall or drinking lite beer. It's child's play. Sure, it's an effective way to shut me off from people and real life, but when a show ends thanks to the aforementioned self-awareness, I immeasurably remember my life. Boo. When Michael and I first moved to Portland, he spent six weeks away for work. Aside from going to meetings and wandering around this strange misty land, I binge watched the fuck out of everything. *Twin Peaks, Veep, Riverdale, Grace and Frankie* and this show called *Greenleaf.* They were all really effective in erasing my life but *Greenleaf* worked the best. I only watched one season but I have to say it was the cocaine of binge watchable shows (jokes, people, jokes.) The show centered on this black family that runs a megachurch in the south. Is running a church even the right word? Like how can you "run" spirituality? Who knows? Anyway, it has Lynn Whitfield as the family matriarch and total bitch, this daughter married to a secretly gay guy who is obsessed with gay dating apps, this weird/gross storyline about the grandpa or uncle being a child molester and Oprah as a sassy aunt who knows the truth and owns a bar! Tell me you're not hooked already! This show provided hours of life melting time and I'm forever grateful to Oprah and the gang. But when I finished the season the fact remained: I was lonely and missing my husband and mildly depressed. It was also not connection with real people. I craved that, I needed that and yet I resisted trying to reach out and get that. I was left with a way to check out but ultimately a life, a few chronic conditions and a brain like mine to deal with.

Sex, porn, jerking off, what have you, are all easy ways to check out but with self-awareness and the brain of an addict it's one slippery, goddamn slope. Oh sure, like any good gay male addict I've tried to dick my way out of life but it's depressing as fuck. Readily available and a reliable high, sex and people in general is an easy fix. It just doesn't last and soon I find myself hunting it down all over again and craving like a crackhead. If you're not careful you can end up in situations that look and feel a lot like the ones you had when you were using. Just as sketchy but without substances to erase it. I don't know if I'd identify as a sex addict but I'm not opposed to the idea. I mean once you've sat in thousands of rooms and told strangers that you're an alcoholic, your defenses come down. Sure, I'm addicted to sex and have 100% without a doubt hit points where my relationship with it has become an issue. Sadly, self-awareness has fucked this one up for me too. Easy hookups are no longer easy and the universe keeps me moving me like a chess piece away from situations that could be a problem. Some of my old ways of checking out have stopped working or being available and this is all for the best. Yet as far as sex goes, I'm not out of the woods and I still have to check my motives with people.

If all of this confessional stuff about still being addicted to nearly everything after several years sober is depressing, I am sorry. I haven't really sold the idea of returning to normal once you find recovery. My old addict brain is still alive and kicking and not going away. I hope yours vanished in the night like a GOP mistress, but mine is still around. However, the silver lining, giant rainbow or whatever happy weather metaphor you prefer, about checking out is I do it a whole lot less.

When I'm really lucky and feeling healthy, I even like feeling regular old non-altered life . Weird, right?!? But it's true. Sometimes the unenhanced existence is more crazy than the checked out one. Not obsessing over something making me feel better is pretty damn weird and magical and wonderful. It's a feeling I should get addicted to too.

Do It Again

FOR THE LOVE of God, can we just talk about Raquel Welch instead of talking about me? Surely, we could have a cup of coffee and blow through 40 minutes just by talking about all the things that didn't happen for Raquel Welch. For example, did you know that she was considered for the role of Alexis on *Dynasty*? Likewise, our dear Raquel was supposed to star in *Cannery Row* but after some major drama (at least 20 minutes' worth of discussion) she was fired. Enter Debra

Winger, which feels like a weird replacement for Raquel, but it was the early 1980's and drugs were a lot stronger back then. She sued, won $10 million dollars and was blackballed. We didn't see her on the screen until 1994. That right there alone could eat some time and we haven't even talked about her foray into pop music with the hit single, *This Girl is Back in Town*. Oh, you didn't know she sang? Well, now you do and we should probably stop and try to find a video of her singing that song or any song, for that matter. Hell, we might even be able to scour YouTube and find her entire variety special, *Raquel!* It could be worth a watch. I hear she does a medley with Tom Jones and a cover of "Games People Play." Or we can just skip to the chase and I could really roll my sleeves up and present you with my theory that her film Kansas City Bomber is actually a feminist classic. This will require about 90 minutes. Hell, I'll even read you a word-by-word recap of a news story from 2012 wherein brave Raquel overcame a finger injury on the set of *CSI: Miami*. It would be my pleasure because the truth of the matter is I talk a lot about myself and it's a little exhausting.

On the surface, it would appear that somebody like me who has been writing about addiction, alcoholism, mental health or some magical combo platter of all three (plus a crunchy taco and frozen margarita for $11.95!) would naturally get tired of talking about all this stuff. Like girl, you've been yammering about this crap for nearly 10 years. Take a break. Honestly, that isn't it. I truly believe that these things I live with-- alcoholism, HIV, addition, depression, etc. - are endless topics. After all, I have to live with them my entire life and as I do whatever the hell it is I do to stay afloat, these enjoyable mental health challenges are simply part of the package. I change, they change and over the years we somehow just figure out how to live with each other. Like Bill and Hillary Clinton. That being said, life through the lens of a person with a brain like mine is surely enough not only for this book but a few more, maybe a TV series and if you're really lucky, a musical ice extravaganza. No, what makes a narcissist like me want to stop talking about themselves is the truth. See, if I embrace the truth and look at where I am, I'm usually not too thrilled at what I find.

Somewhere around my seventh year sober, I started to act really entitled about this whole self-awareness and self-improvement garbage. Wasn't there some spiritual growth guest list where I didn't have to stand in line and do the work of actually feeling better? Haven't I grown enough already? Surely, someone worse off could use the growth more than me? Moreover, hadn't I already done enough to stay sober and sane? Didn't all those hours, all those meeting count for something? Apparently not and also this would be considered resting on my laurels which to be honest doesn't sound that bad. I enjoy rest and from what I've been able to gather Laurel, whoever she is, is okay with us resting on her. Where's the harm?

I bristle when people--those people I seek out for advice like my therapist, my sponsor, and sober friends- point this out to me." Maybe you just need to work a tiny bit harder," a friend of mine told me years ago when I had yet another patch of spiritual dryness. This annoyed the crap out of me. Sure, I had asked him what I should do, but that's not the answer I wanted. I wanted him to applaud my efforts so far and maybe even buy me an Americano. And a cookie. Yeah that wouldn't have given me any spiritual clarity, but I'll take a shallow pat on the back, accompanied by a baked good and coffee in lieu of actual life solutions any day of the week. But my friend, in this instance, was correct. This isn't to say I did actually work a tiny bit harder, but it was advice I've carried with me for years.

But I didn't want to do the work because--hello- it's work. Let it be known that I am not a huge fan of work even though, in a professional sense, I've been working since I was 13. I've even been called a "hard worker" which is something I'm also not that thrilled about. For decades, I've been trying to carefully craft the polar opposite of being a hard worker. I'd like to be sitting under a shady tree and drinking lemonade as the world brings stuff to me. Hard worker in the sheets, aspiring lady of leisure on the streets.

Yet with the kind of work I need to do to stay sober, sane and basically not a total nightmare, I don't have a choice. I guess I do but that choice involves me relapsing and losing my mind (again) so I have to rally. For me, the work in question involves going to meetings, seeing my therapist, helping other drunks and drug addicts and trying to muster up some sort of non-denominational but effective spiritual life. When I first got sober, my mangled, delusional ass was willing to do whatever work you told me to do, just as long as there was some kind of promise that maybe I'd feel better and want to stop dying. I'd show up early to places. I'd call random people. I'd make coffee for angry addicts who had a lot of opinions about how and when said free coffee should happen. I really would do anything you told me to, partially because I wanted to stay sober and of course I wanted people to like me. In this case, my endless seeking of approval served me well.

But then it all gets tricky because it all gets good; it meaning life. I married someone awesome and was actually getting paid to write. I felt healthy. I didn't argue with the people in the middle of Sunset Blvd anymore. I knew where my phone was most of the time. Like I said, good. The minute things get good, my brain tells me to stop doing the work. To take a break, to kick my feet up. To stop calling other drunks. And stop making coffee for feisty sober folks. Then, it goes from good to terrifying pretty fast. How long do I listen to that voice until I think I don't need it show up at all anymore? Before I know it, I'll forego the lemonade and shady tree and just head back to the dive bar with shots. Or even worse- I won't drink and just be insane instead.

I'm not proud to say, and go ahead and revoke my Sober Beacon of Light Award, but I have been there in sobriety. A few times. My addict brain has a built in magnet to misery and anytime it feels even the slightest pull, I can be dragged towards it, sometimes without me even knowing. I wound up there at two years sober. I briefly visited there at 4 years. I showed up back there at 8 years. Each time, I land in a place where my world shrinks and my hope fizzles. I don't necessarily want to drink or use drugs but jumping in front of a bus doesn't sound like the worst idea ever either. To makes things even more uncomfortable, I soon start to feel indignant, resentful and superior. In short, I'm a fucking delight to be around. My brain tells me that I don't need help anymore. I've got this. Soon, too soon, I've fallen off the things that made me feel good in the first place and now it feels far away. My pride gets in the way of wanting to go back and ask for help, yet by some freaking miracle, I have been able to navigate my way back to what worked before I've fallen completely off the rails.

Call it survival instinct. Call it faith. Call it whatever, but I am lucky enough to have decided to go back again to what worked in the beginning, in those days where I was desperate and I just needed relief. This is where the truth comes back in and where I can't hide behind

Raquel Welch. Although she did once say, "I'm far more ready to go with the flow now because I am more accepting of myself." When I head back to the start and go back to what helped in my early recovery, I have to yet again get honest about how I'm living and behaving. Groan. Usually, it's in this process where I find something, some part of me, which is no longer working.

Currently, I am back in the work of recovery and what's reared its ugly head is my propensity for shit talking, gossiping and good old fashioned character assassination. Being the toughest talking, smartass bitch in the room was kind of my preordained role and a role that helped me survive. Zingers, jokes and insults sometimes got me out of really tense situations. Plus this all was part of my identity. I had already gotten rid of the being wasted part. If this was to go, what would be left? If I'm not talking shit, who even am I?

Yet I feel ready to let it go because I've learned through decades of trial and error, that the more I push to feel better, the closer I get to being somebody who I like. Therefore, I do it all again. Not because it's the only way, but it's the way that worked for me and because I'm uncomfortable as fuck. So, I call the random people again. I read the stuff and write the stuff they tell me to again. I show up to meetings and things I don't want to show to again. And I make the coffee for picky people in recovery again. Because although I haven't relapsed in the time I've been sober, I certainly have felt like shit. I definitely have felt the moments that were once bright get dark and that's something I don't want to do again.

A Little Respect

PART WOOD NYMPH, part rock star, the mere sight of Andy Bell in short shorts and wearing a flower crown undoubtedly changed me. Throughout the concert, he was flanked by two fierce black backup singers also covered in glitter and flowers. It was like a Renaissance painting did ecstasy while watching Little Shop of Horrors and decided to put on a show. And what a show it was. I was 16 years old and here was this rare, gay man out and proud and having a huge musical career in 1990 while I was a closeted, burgeoning drug addict who didn't even know who I was. Bell was almost too much to look at. So in-your-face, so sweet, so charming and so out of fucks to give, it seemed like the me that could be, but a me that was totally out of reach. I mean, Andy Bell was the lead singer of Erasure and I was just some effeminate teenager in Golden, Colorado.

Bullied, beaten up and black and blue, I ran towards anything that looked shinier and more beautiful than the existence I had as a teenager. It wasn't just music like Erasure's but Bowie, Sinead O'Connor, Deee-Lite, Madonna and anything else I could dance to and forget who I was. Drugs fit fabulously into this plan too. When I was high, I didn't have to feel the pains of growing up gay in an alcoholic home. When I was with the kids I used with, I was cool, not just some kid that got routinely called faggot as he walked down the hall. I wasn't the kid you pushed in the cafeteria because he wouldn't push back; I was a smart ass drunk and drug addict who could drink you under the table. I was cool or at the very least cool adjacent. I knew who to hang out with to at least give the appearance of being cool. I was also a kid with an incredible taste in music. Drinking, drugs and listening to cassette tapes or going to teen alternative clubs was basically my whole life. Instead of being in class, I was smoking cloves dancing to "Personal Jesus", drinking Big Gulps spiked with whiskey and watching Book of Love in concert. I was taking drugs and seeing Love and Rockets, and smoking weed and singing Madonna at Burger King. I had no use for traditional school, a place where I was regularly fucked with for being who I was. Instead, I sought out personal enrichment through drugs, pop culture and music. Why go to biology when you can take acid, listen to New Order and go to the mall? Perpetually in peril and in over my head with a life out of control, almost anybody who knew me, who didn't do drugs with me, was probably concerned about me. People of all kinds tried to help or tried to figure out what was wrong but to no avail. After all, I was a nice kid, a creative kid and a kid who couldn't fit with everybody else no matter how hard he tried. I couldn't even be invisible, which was a real bitch. Okay, fine. I'll be the gayest child that Colorado ever saw in 1989, but can I at least camouflage into the background?

Yet that was not my story. I was extra before we even started saying extra. Therefore the "extra" artists of that era- Erasure, Cyndi Lauper, Pete Burns, Boy George- forged the path for me to walk down. But what did I do when I wasn't listening to music or dancing or going to concerts? It's not like Andy Bell could magically appear like the fairy from Pinocchio and perform Blue Savannah every time I felt horrible. Likewise, giving myself platinum blonde hair like Madonna wasn't a real substitution for self-esteem, although it didn't stop me from trying. Drugs and alcohol, thank god, gave me the ability to not give a fuck, like Mr. Bell himself. After spending my junior year harassed and pushed around, I emerged my senior year of high school as some kind of faux phoenix. The kids who fucked with me the most had graduated and now I could smoke cigarettes, talk shit, get high and listen to music in my friend's cars without caring who hated me. Sure, I was still teased but after a summer of going to gay clubs, doing acid and dancing all night long, as directed by Miss Cathy Dennis, I had developed a swagger that sort of looked like self-esteem. I tried my best to own who I was but without actually being out of the closet or actually liking myself; it was just a performance.

A long running performance, at that. A tough exterior of joke cracking gay best friend who knew all the cool kids served me well all the way into my thirties. But the thing about that kid who knows all the good bands and has gossipy stories about celebrities and bitchy take downs of coworkers is that's all there is to him. My inability to get real about the hurt, sadness, shame and self-hate that I felt inside 24 hours a day was killing me. Towards the end, drugs and alcohol didn't just loosen up the act and make life more comfortable, they were vital for even leaving the house. I hated myself and no amount of male pop stars in hot pants could make that go away.

At age 45 and counting, I am now unable to suppress a deep sigh or at the bare minimum a low-key eye roll when people flippantly say, "Love yourself." Undoubtedly catchy for some other generation to enjoy in a Justin Bieber song, the idea of loving yourself to a person like me sounds downright puzzling. "Love yourself!" and while you're at it solve world hunger.

Love yourself. Please. As if someone merely telling us to love ourselves is enough. In fact, a lot of times when people say "They need to love themselves" it's a way to comment on the perceived low self-esteem of others. Love yourself, you pathetic mess. Even Rupaul's well-intended and much quoted, "If you can't love yourself, how in the hell you gonna love somebody else?" is a loaded shortcut to something that I've found very hard to do. Trying to love myself sounds a little easier, while liking myself more than I did before, is sometimes really the best I can muster.

In 2010, a good 20 years after I had the magical gay epiphany of seeing Andy Bell and Erasure on stage, the band once again entered my conscience. A year and a half sober, I was visiting my sister and her kids in Colorado. The place I had grown up in had changed too- thanks marijuana! It was no longer the deep red state steeped in homophobia and hatred. It had come around a little and so had I. My niece and nephew, who possess not just great sets of eyelashes, but incredible senses of humor, were obsessed with the video game "Robot Unicorn Attack." The ridiculous game had its moment in the sun as sort of a viral obsession and along with it came an Erasure reemergence. The band's song "Always" is winkingly featured as the game's theme song. Quick to pick up on anything amazing, my niece and nephew loved the song too. They'd giggle uncontrollably when Bell would dramatically sing, "Open your eyes. Your eyes are open." It seemed all too perfect that this band and this song would show back up at a point where I was starting to like myself.

Now aged 50-something with his hot pants days behind him, Andy Bell is sober too. He's talked openly, like we would expect anything less, about his battle with drugs and alcohol. There's something comforting about knowing that this gay icon who was utterly 100% himself maybe hated himself too and that makes his role in who I grew up to be even more profound. It makes the beautiful angel whose music I loved on friends' cassette tapes relatable and real, Perhaps Andy Bell, like the rest of us, faked loving himself, until he could get close to the real thing.

Maybe that's the best any of us can do? Maybe we should take this ultimatum of "love yourself or fail at life" off the table completely. Because what I know is all of this-this feeling better, this trying to stop killing myself, this path to even tolerating myself, much less loving myself- it's a lot of fucking work. No amount of Bieber songs or stickers or mugs or even *Drag Race* episodes can make me love myself. It's a long road I have to walk (and occasionally fall off) every day. Being the good drug addict that I am, it's unfortunate to discover I can't snort self-esteem like I used to snort cocaine. Instead, self-esteem and yeah, even loving myself comes in little doses through small efforts. Just not being a dick to people at the grocery store. Holding the door open for someone and not expecting a round of applause. And not using drugs or alcohol one day at a goddamn time get me closer. Closer to a little more happiness, a little more self-esteem and even a little respect.

What to Say When Someone Next To You Is OD'ing

LIKE MOST REASONABLE people at some point in their

lives, the other day I wondered, "What would Carol

Hathaway do?" What would the nurse, played by

Julianna Margulies on six seasons of the television

drama *ER* do if she, in her pink scrubs, wound up where I was the other day? How would Carol handle a person dying from a drug overdose right next to her? Well, Carol is a nurse, granted a pretend nurse on a cancelled TV show, but a nurse nonetheless, which still makes her more of a medical professional than me. So Carol would do nursey things, things that were helpful and lifesaving. And the other day I couldn't do those things. What's more, I could barely figure out what to say when all of this was unfolding right before me at a crazy pace. I'm sure good old Carol would say something comforting as well, but the best I could come up with the other day as a man was overdosing right next to me was, "Call 911."

When I think about moments like this potentially happening, my obvious point of reference is television.

It'll be heroic and a moment of my own personal strength! It'll be like that scene in season 4 of *Grey's Anatomy* where Izzie, as played by Katherine Heigl, does mouth-to-mouth on a dying deer. Well, it was none of those things. I didn't feel heroic, just scared and awful. Trust me, I would have rather been Katherine Heigl that day and I'm pretty sure I'm the only person ever to write those words. It all happened so terrifyingly fast, as things often do at my non-writer mental health and addictions based day job. But this day, with someone's life in peril, was a first.

Listen, I can't tell all of his story due to the nature of my job and it's actually not really about that. It's about me. I mean, I'm an alcoholic. Of course I can make someone else's overdose all about me! But I will say that this person, like me, has struggled his whole life with drugs and alcohol. Lots of times in my job I get to see people, who also like me, finally overcome these things and change their lives. More often than not, however, I get to see the really hard stuff. Wednesday was one of those days.

After talking to him and trying to just keep him awake, the paramedics showed up. They arrived really quickly, and despite having to use Wikipedia (!!!!!!) to figure out what Suboxone was (in a state with a major heroin crisis, mind you), they were fantastic. They did all the nursey Carol Hathaway things I couldn't do... or maybe all the things an EMT character on that show would do. I stopped watching after Clooney left, so I don't know who that would be. Anyway, they wheeled him off on a stretcher, slid him into the ambulance and sped away. What they didn't take with them was poor, shattered ill-equipped, non-nursey me.

With lump in throat and tears waiting in the wings to fall from my face, I decided that this was probably a good moment to call it a day. I needed to go collapse in the privacy of my own home where my husband and cats could be on call to pick up the pieces. I think it affected me so deeply because for one, I am a human being. Sounds like a stupid thing to even type but as a drunken, drug taking robot on a suicide mission for 20 years, I need to write that from time to time. A human watching another human in peril SHOULD be upsetting and my response felt appropriate. Again, it sounds crazy to even justify that but as an addict who used to live in a constant state of "I'M FINE. I'M FINE. I'M FINE" just to admit a normal emotional response is still liberating. Now, at the workplace, I've got to keep it together. Nobody wants a mental health professional bursting into tears. What would Carol Hathaway think?! But in the comfort of my own world, with the people I trust, it felt okay to not be fucking okay.

It also affected me because I am an addict and for a moment I thought, "This could be me" followed by the guilt-induced but totally honest thought, "Thank god it isn't me." The thing is every time someone relapses or overdoses or god forbid dies, we all think this. We all think that could be/should be me followed by, I'm so glad that it isn't. It's the ghost of Alcoholic Christmas Future right in front of your face, telling you this is what waits for you if you decide to go back. The obtuse "What If?" worst case scenario became tangible in that moment as this guy, this usually funny, charming, energetic guy nearly slipped away right next to me. For lack of a more poetic turn of phrase, it sucked.

What really hit me in those rushed few moments that felt like a shook up Coke bottle about to explode, this guy was a human too. Somebody's son. Somebody's friend. Somebody's dad. He wasn't a HuffPo article or CNN statistic about the opioid epidemic. He was a living breathing example of what it looks like today all across the country. Luckily, I saw this human being yesterday at the hospital. He is doing okay. As I told him what happened the last time we saw each other, he looked shocked and apologized several times. I told him it was okay and then I did what Carol Hathaway couldn't do: laugh with him as a fellow addict. I told him it was a good thing we weren't using at the same time otherwise we'd both be in the hospital. I told him to play nice with the other kids at rehab. I told him yes, we still had all of his stuff and we'd hang onto it. Mainly, I tried to tell him, "I get it," because I honestly do and because over and over again in my recovery, people have told me they get it too.

Traumarama

I THINK ON some level when you have a gun pointed in your face, you have to think, "This will probably mess me up later." It might occur to you that this kid robbing you wasn't just running off with $300 dollars, but probably running off with a piece of your soul too. You may even have the insight to consider that this simple Saturday night robbery could cause you trauma somewhere down the road. After all, this is a fucked up and scary thing to happen. You're lucky to have gotten out of it alive. You might need a minute to process it and feel better and you might even think about getting some help around it. Well, you might but I didn't.

This actual thing that happened to me in the year Two Thousand and Alcoholism was legitimately scary. But in that moment, I didn't have time to feel it. "I didn't have time to feel it" is basically what this essay collection should have been called because, like every other messed up or life altering event, this robbery, this assault, this attack was shoved into a corner. In my defense, however, I had to rush home to somebody else's emergency (somebody else's emergency is what my book on codependency should be called). My boyfriend at the time had been in a car accident. He was the one in peril, not me. I'd be fine, I'd bounce back. Didn't I always? No, actually but at least I'd fake like everything was okay and hope to god you didn't notice how bad off I really was. As far as Saturday night's go, this one sucked.

The worst thing about getting mugged that night was knowing it was about to go down. I worked at a restaurant in Silver Lake in Los Angeles at the time. I walked to and from that place dozens of times and had it down to a science. I knew what side of Sunset Blvd felt safe and which shortcut through the neighborhood would get me home fastest. But that night, for some reason I still don't know, I forgot those things. That night I stayed on the poorly lit, sketchier side of the street which in Los Angeles is really subjective. I mean, once you've stepped over the body of a guy who got shot on your patio, your definition of sketchy is decidedly high bar. Nevertheless, that Saturday night I forgot all of those things and walked where I shouldn't and the minute I heard footprints behind me, I knew I was fucked. He was with other people. Or I think he was. There might have been a van that he hopped out of. It's all kind of fuzzy. I held onto the wallet and just gave him the cash which was considerable after a night of waiting tables. I knew just handing it over was the only thing to do. I ignored my street sense earlier and I wound up here. Now was not the time to bust out some karate moves (that I didn't know). Getting shot seemed like it would really be inconvenient for everybody involved. This 17 year-old didn't actually want to shoot me and probably didn't even think that far in advance. I certainly didn't want it either. I was already annoyed. A gunshot wound would really send my annoyance over the edge. Honestly, a deep feeling of being irritated is what I remember from the whole night. When I finally got home, I was thrown into a drunken drama of my ex and our friend who all acted like their fender bender was the great tragedy of Two Thousand and Alcoholism. It wasn't just annoying being robbed but then I was unheard, uncomfortable and unnoticed in the moment. Day drinking, shopping and movie the next day was my strategy to forget and move on and honestly I thought I had.

Some 12 years later, 9 years of them spent sober and trying to sort this kind of shit out, I realized I wasn't okay. It pushed me to walk cautiously for sure but it also made me not trust people with things I felt were traumatic. I'd keep that stuff to myself. I'd leave it all in the dark. I'd drink to numb it. So, when all of those techniques are gone, then what the hell are you supposed to do? Deal with it is the unfortunate answer. Last May in the year Two Thousand And Sober, I felt rattled. Violence from childhood showed up in my thoughts after a weekend with family. It wasn't just a gun in my face on Sunset Blvd; it was deeper. Old ghosts from my old life that I thought had gone away because, god dammit, I was sober and in recovery and therefore totally okay, right? were back. They were back and those bitches wanted some answers. They wanted to know why they were still around. They wanted to know what I was going to do about it.

These ghosts told the story of a childhood filled with violence and uncertainty. Growing up in an alcoholic home is like growing up on a battlefield. Coming home from school, holidays, family dinners were always peppered with the possibility that everything could go from zero to bonkers in a matter of seconds. Like, damn I thought we were just having mashed potatoes and all of a sudden, they're being flung across the room. Event after event happens and soon as a kid this sort of chaos just becomes how you and your family roll. Oh, you mean you haven't seen your dad pour a beer on your mom's head? Weird. Nevertheless, when I took a drink at 14 years old, I was READY. I had seen some shit already and I needed a cocktail or 40 to take the edge off. While we're at it take all the edges off. Bust out the edge clippers. I really liked acid as a 15 year old because it made existence really otherworldly. Sure, it was scary and things could go really bad really quickly. But the world while on acid could never be as scary as the one I grew up in and at least when I was on acid, I forgot who I was and where I came from. Besides, it made things like math class and going to the mall a lot more entertaining. If you haven't hallucinated in front of a Merry Go Round, have you even lived? But just like the cocktails after being mugged, whatever I tried to do as a kid to get rid of it didn't work especially the longer I stayed sober.

The "it" in question here is trauma. In my non-writer life where I work with addicts and alcoholics , trauma is the word medical and mental health professionals alike say over and over again. I wonder if we almost say it too much. We use it to explain everything so much that maybe it dulls out how painful and shitty trauma is to live with? Regardless, some crazy numbers are thrown around too when we talk about trauma and addiction, but in lieu of having those at the ready I'll step out on a ledge here and say nearly every damn person with a drug or alcohol problem also has some kind of trauma.

The more I talk to people like me, the more I realize they've seen what I've seen or worse. Trauma levels the playing field with people in recovery. We're all meeting each other from a place of damage. It's a shitty place to have in common, but damn, at least we don't have to be there alone. The times where my heads nods as someone I'm working with shares what they've been through are too numerous to count. My nodding heads says, "yes", "yes', "me too" and "you're not alone." They've been through "it" and so I have I, even if my "it" is different from theirs. There's no trauma dance off or competition to see who's worse off. We've individually seen some shit and now we get to see some different shit.

A low bar goal of mine, as a sober person, is to not further traumatize people. It's the least I can do. From fellow bar patrons and poor, worried family members to cab drivers and neighbors, I am sure I have played a role in more than a few traumas. Best supporting actress in a trauma. It doesn't seem like a big deal I guess, when you have a million little traumas of your own that you're running from. Like I'm filled with trauma, so let me just take you hostage to this trauma party. Now, I recognize my shit and I try to keep others out of it. I know where the damage comes from. Moreover, I know what happens when I ignore it. I dance a little PTSD dance where I shout back to ghosts while trying learning to live with them. "GO AWAY," I yell. "Or stay but just keep it down." Unrecognized and undealt with traumas have long been these unsettled stories that I don't understand. Are they still painful? Uh yeah. Did they leave a mark? More than a few. But in the year Two Thousand And Sober Now, I'm no longer afraid to look at them.

Cry With a Stranger

ON THURSDAY NIGHTS at 6:30pm in Northwest Portland, in a beautiful blue old Victorian home, for the last half a year or so, I go hang out with a stranger and cry. The first time, back in late November (or was it early December? Time flies when you're crying with someone you barely know.), it took me all of about 35 minutes to burst into tears. Maybe it was the slight grandma vibe of the room or maybe it was the fact that he didn't seem like the type to be rattled by a bawling gay man in his forties but there it was. Me and this stranger, my new therapist, wading through my tears. Now, I don't go there just to cry. It would be freaking weird if that was my thing, my kink. Getting off on paying strangers and having them make me cry. That's some freaky shit but whatever floats your boat. I guess I could sort of get why crying would be someone's thing. It's always been really freeing for me. I was criticized for doing it too much as kid, only to discover in my 20's that my beloved grandpa Bob was a renowned and fearless crier from way back when. In what sounds like the worst seminar that middle aged white men from Seattle would attend in the woods, I guess you could say over the years I've reclaimed crying for myself. In early sobriety, the tears would just fall. I even had a playlist that would help push tears out of my eyes. It was basically Godspeed by Jenny Lewis and a bunch of other stuff that helped my Godspeed cry keep going. That song made me cry so many times, I feel like I should send her some money too. Oh God. Maybe crying is my kink? Anyway, the longer I stay sober, I see the value in it but I wasn't in this quaint little office in a Victorian attic just to cry, thank you very much. I was here because I felt like I was in trouble. Not in trouble with the law or my parents or my bosses, but in peril of the emotional variety.

After years sober, I still felt broken. Time with my family stirred it up while time away from them pushed it to the forefront. I was also working in the new stressful and intense world of mental health and addiction, which is how I framed it when I spoke to him on the phone. You know just to learn how to deal with the stress and learn how to process the things I saw and dealt with. The truth was, there were still a lot of old stories and old events that hurt to even think about much less talk about. Sure, I'd done a lot of work in my recovery around some of that stuff, but the residual damage left by a childhood in an alcoholic home, trauma caused by an abusive relationship and other terrifying tales left me feeling incomplete. Here I was sober for all of these years, but my insides still were mixed up and deeply sad. These were the kind of ghosts a 12 Step program or a fellow addict couldn't take care of. I need to call in a professional.

The jig was up during our first visit. I had some shit and he needed to help me figure out what this shit was. Minutes after I sat down, I told him that I was addicted to approval to which he replied, "Well you're not going to get it from me in this space." He wasn't having my bullshit in the most compassionate way possible and I loved him already. I didn't need a therapist who was going to be my fan. I needed someone who would help me find the truth. We decided I would come every week. Each session was hard and filled with more crying. I often found myself wondering, "Why am I looking at painful shit from my past? Why am I causing more trouble for myself?" I didn't know why and I really was rethinking the entire idea for the first month.

Here's a hot tip about therapy: maybe not dive deep into childhood trauma around the holidays and your upcoming sober anniversary? Maybe wait for a sleepier, less triggery season because all I know is that "the most wonderful time of the year" in 2017 was filled with a lot of crying in the shower and discovering new versions of "Have Yourself a Merry Little Christmas" to bawl over while walking around the mall. Lamely, I tried to get into the spirit. I baked so many cookies for so many people. Our apartment looked like Martha Stewart and Santa were getting ready for an orgy. I tried to find a holiday movie (or forty) to ease the pain. Nothing worked. The fact was, I was freshly heartbroken, which is an odd thing to say because the events I was crying over were all decades old.

I remember tearfully telling my therapist that I was sad and not sad just because some hard, violent, shitty things had happened to me. But sad for me. I was sad for that the little kid version of me that had to go through that, sad that kid got beat up, And sad that kid got knocked down and never got up. Mainly, I was really sad for big old alcoholic, drug addict me for trying the best he could to wipe it all from his conscious to no avail. All this sadness meant more crying. I cried myself a wave that knocked me off that grandma couch and outside that quaint little Victorian house. The tears carried me down the street and back to my shower. But while all this crying was happening, other stuff was happening too. Forgiveness, acceptance and weird peace that I didn't expect.

Sure, I still wasn't exactly sure why I was here every Thursday stirring up trouble but, I felt better too. Turns out your heart can shatter and you can cry for an entire holiday season and somehow be okay. Better than okay, I was stronger than yesterday, Britney. This stranger helped me see that I was a lot stronger than I ever gave myself credit for and therefore looking at all of this stuff wasn't scary. It was the opposite; it was freedom. The things I lived through didn't haunt me or destroy me. They gave me a strength I didn't know I had and this stranger helped me find that.

I still had tears left to cry, Ariana. There were certainly more tear-filled therapy sessions in the future. There was a possibility I'd spend next Christmas crying too. Or I could be like grandpa Bob and cry at the drop of a hat for the rest of my life. But if I was lucky, I'd continue to just let the tears fall.

Thanks for Letting Me Cher

ONE NIGHT IN 2009, when I had about 6 months sober, I was leaving a meeting in Santa Monica and I heard it coming from an SUV. It was a familiar, campy jingle jangle intro of a seventies song I had heard about 4,000 times since childhood. "I was born in a wagon of a travelling show. My mama used to dance for the money they'd throw," she sang. *Of course* I was leaving a gay meeting that night and *of course* it was a Cher song. I had to laugh out loud the minute I heard it. *Gypsies, Tramps and Thieves.* Perfect. That title pretty much describes all of the attendees of every 12 Step meeting I've ever been to. Clearly, I was in the right place.

Having grown up in more of the Madonna generation than the Cher-Barbra-Bette era of young gay men, the diva was already on her 750th comeback by the time she won her Oscar, when I was a teenager. It was hard not to love Cher even though I was more of a goth- new wave kid and she was recoding Bon Jovi in fishnets music at the time. Cher was an outsider, a rebel and she didn't care. Those were all things I aspired to be, so she was added to the lengthy list of celebrities I was obsessed about in 1989. As I got older and into my mid-twenties, Cher had her 751st comeback with "Believe" and I was fully out of the closet both as a gay man and Cher obsessive. The closest I ever got to the Cher-o-sphere in person was when I was 28 and working at a clothing company. Per the request of her stylist, I sent Cher some samples of the arm bands and gloves that we made. She sent me back a signed cd, which meant we were basically best friends.

I also saw her in concert as part of her farewell tour that wasn't really a farewell tour in 2005. This concert is harder to remember. Hard to remember because I was wasted drunk during that concert, so every detail is fuzzy. It wasn't just hard to remember, it was difficult because it still kind of stings. Here was this diva I loved for years and I barely remember a thing about that concert. I blacked out somewhere after *Take Me Home* and before *Heart of Stone*. I was sloppy drunk and it was an evening I regretted even before it was over. I do remember having drinks before the concert with my best friend and a random couple we met; they were excited that The Village People were opening for Cher. "I can't wait to do the YMCA for real," the woman said. "I've only done it at weddings and bar mitzvahs!" I also remember the men's restroom being the cruisiest gay spot I'd ever been to outside of a San Francisco leather bar. Other than that, I got nothing. Which is too bad. I really wish I had a magical Cher moment to pass onto you, but I do not. I will however take this opportunity to discourage anyone who thinks drinking a lot and walking down the hills of the Hollywood Bowl sounds like a fun idea. It isn't. Ugh. What a mess. I think I owe myself a Cher amends at some point.

Back in the rooms of recovery of 2009, I hope I would have made Cher proud. After all, she's a self-professed member of Al-Anon, presumably after being married to Greg Allman. However, Allman was such an accomplished alcoholic that I think even if you purchased his greatest hits, you'd qualify for Al-Anon. But more than that, I hope I embraced the honesty that my idol had always proudly displayed. She always said what was on her mind and now I needed to do the same if I wanted to stay sober. To be fair, I didn't learn how to share in meetings from Cher; I learned it from other alcoholics and addicts.

Week after week, meeting after meeting, I would hear people share about trying to stay sober when life got bad. We lost a member of our group who died of cancer, but died sober. We lost others who relapsed.

We lost a few to suicide. We also had people stay sober through good times like job promotions, weddings and financial successes. You know the kind of things you'd drink over to celebrate. People share about that too. I remember complaining once to my sponsor about a guy who bitched every week about his neighbors. To which my sponsor replied, "Well, he's not drinking over his neighbors, now is he?" Fair point.

I also noticed that the people who really shared, were the ones who stayed and stayed sober. The others who sat silently? Not so much. Being "wonderfully verbal" as a friend of mine once described me, I tried to jump right into sharing at meetings. I ALWAYS had something to say and I was sure that it was genius. I was also sure everyone else was obsessed with what I shared too. One night after a meeting and after a long and scattered share, I said to my friend, "I hope my share made sense." Totally deadpan, he replied, "You shared tonight?" When I picked up a year, another friend said, "you're a lot less crazy than you were when you got here!' Turns out, my shares weren't that memorable. But I was feeling better. For the first time ever, I was trying to come clean about what was really happening. I was sharing about all the things I never wanted anyone to know for fear that I would be ridiculed. But as time went on, the reverse happened. The harder something was to talk about, the more it connected me to others. When I got my HIV diagnosis at seven moths sober, I shared about it. Immediately, tons of gay men from my homegroup rallied around me. They told me they were positive too. They told me I was going to be okay. They told me where to go to get meds. They told me I didn't have to drink over it. And I believed them. Shame, lies and self-hate drove me to the brink of death and now sharing the truth had brought me back to life. It was a comeback of my own that surely Cher would approve of.

In the cult classic Burlesque, Cher sings *You Haven't Seen the Last of Me*. The song, like *Gypsies, Tramps and Thieves* could be for every alcoholic too. Those of us who fought to stay alive and stay sober feel it in our bones when La Cher sings, "I am down, but I'll get up again." But I won't unless, I open my mouth. Each time, I write or speak or podcast or even share at a meeting, I'm fighting to stay honest and to stay here. The more I tell my story and tell on myself, the less power my alcoholism and addiction have.

So sadly, no you haven't seen or heard the last of me,

but I hope I haven't seen the last of you either.

Acknowledgments

There are so many beautiful people who helped get this little volume into your hands that "acknowledgments" hardly seems to be sufficient of a word for what they've contributed. But it's what The Book People call it so until we can come up with a better word, I'd like to acknowledge my face off.

Michael: You take the daily brunt of living on the set of *The Sean Show* and you do it with considerable love, humor and grace. You are my best friend, the love of my life and you make me want to be a better writer and human being. Also, thank you for feeding the cats when I was too self-involved to remember to do so.

Anna David: Your magic as writer, a hustler and a human truly made this project happen. You also gave me the sage advice of "try being less earnest" and by doing so you have unleashed a sassy sarcastic beast that cannot be contained and I'm forever in your debt.

Paul Fuhr: Your unwavering support and belief in me is above and beyond as a publisher. You took this work sight unseen and I hope I did you proud. I am honored to work with you and call you a friend.

Claire Foster: Thanks for the walks, the importu coaching sessions, the pastries and for turning me on to the simple genius of note cards.

My family: You were the first people to laugh at my jokes so if anyone out there thinks this book isn't at all funny, you are to blame. But seriously, I love you all so much and thank you for the exhausting task of living with and encouraging a lifelong storyteller.

My Online Sober Family: For nearly 8 years, you magnificent creatures have read my shit when no one else would. You told me to keep writing, you told me to keep sharing and when need be you told me to get over myself. You also inspired me wiht your own amazing work and my career in this space would not exist without you. This book was created with you in mind.

My In-Person Sober Family: Day to day, you do the stuff you need to do stay sober, to stay alive and to stay available for me and so many others. You inspire me to try to do the same. I would actually be dead without you. I had you all on my mind when I wrote these essays and I can't wait to hear what you think. I'll buy the iced coffees.

49104290R00249

Made in the USA
San Bernardino, CA
20 August 2019